UN:
The First Ten Years

by

CLARK M. EICHELBERGER

Foreword by JAMES T. SHOTWELL

This book, by one of the men who helped to prepare the first American draft of the UN Charter, shows the evolution of the United Nations in a rapidly changing world, points out its successes and failures in the first decade of its existence, and makes specific recommendations for improving its operations. The question of Charter review, which comes up automatically in 1955, is studied in the light of recent history.

At least four major developments have taken place since the United Nations was created in San Francisco in 1945, against which its success must be measured: the break-up of the five-power system, the development of thermo-nuclear fission, the rapid liquidation of a major part of the colonial system, and the doctrine of economic and social advancement through technical assistance.

Mr. Eichelberger believes that without the United Nations the world could not have survived the tremendous and revolutionary developments of the last nine years. Citing from the record, he weighs the accomplishments of the UN in peaceful settlement, collective security, protection of independent peoples, human rights and economic advancement. He shows to what extent these have been brought about by a broad interpretation and resourceful implementation of the Charter. At the same time, he points out

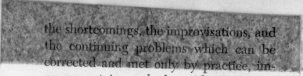

the shortcomings, the improvisations, and the continuing problems which can be corrected and met only by practice, improvement in methods, or finally by revision of the Charter itself.

But most important to the proper functioning of the UN is the attitude of its members. So far, few governments have fulfilled their obligations to the UN completely and without reservations. It is not so much the Charter that has fallen short, the author believes, as the courage and imagination of the people and their governments. Until each nation is willing to regard the United Nations as the foundation rather than the instrument of its foreign policy, the full purpose of the UN will not be realized, and the world will continue on the brink of disaster.

Of this book, Eleanor Roosevelt says:

"A very clear and valuable record of the first ten years of the UN. There will, of course, be differences of opinion about the author's evaluations, but he has been connected with so much of the development of the UN that what he has to say is of great interest."

For the past twenty-five years CLARK M. EICHELBERGER has held important positions in such groups as the League of Nations Association and the Commission to Study the Organization of Peace. In 1942, he was one of a committee of five who prepared the first American draft of the UN Charter. In 1945, he acted as a consultant to the U.S. delegation at the San Francisco Conference. Executive Director of the American Association for the United Nations, he devotes much time to writing and lecturing about the UN.

UN: The First Ten Years

U N:
THE FIRST
TEN YEARS

by
CLARK M. EICHELBERGER

HARPER & BROTHERS, PUBLISHERS
New York

TO THE MEMORY OF MY FATHER

Contents

Acknowledgments

This volume represents an effort to present in a few bold strokes a picture of the development of the United Nations against the background of the major crises with which it has had to deal. I will be satisfied if I have helped some people see the United Nations as an evolving international society in which the American people and their government must play a very important part. This volume is not intended to be a detailed history of the United Nations. I am aware of how many important points, such as the use of the International Court of Justice, have had to be omitted or referred to altogether too briefly.

I am indebted to many people for whatever good ideas are in this volume. One's views are really a composite of the views of many associates. I am indebted to many associates in the American Association for the United Nations and its research affiliate, the Commission to Study the Organization of Peace. Nevertheless I take sole responsibility for the opinions expressed herein.

I am indebted to those who have gone over the manuscript, particularly Professor Quincy Wright of the University of Chicago for his patience in making many important suggestions and corrections. I wish to thank my colleague Margaret Olson. Her exceptional memory of ideas that have been discussed by our associates for many years and her thorough knowledge of the United Nations have been invaluable aids

Foreword

By JAMES T. SHOTWELL

This is an illuminating and thoughtful study of the most
challenging political institution of our time, or, for that matter, of any time. This rapid but authoritative review of a
decade of United Nations' history deals with so many problems of familiar public debate that the central fact behind
them all tends to be forgotten. It is that never until our time
was the elimination of war, as such, a practical problem of
governments. It was accepted in international law as a legitimate instrument of policy, the oldest, most potent of all such
instruments. The challenge to this concept, made by the
League of Nations in its Protocol of Geneva in 1924, was
only half-heartedly accepted and then finally overthrown for
a while by the Axis Powers in their conspiracy against the
peace. But in the Charter of the United Nations the pledge
against war has no loophole such as had been left in the
Covenant of the League, and for a time it seemed as though
a solid renunciation of war had been guaranteed by the Great
Powers. Ten years of history show two sobering facts: the
Communist Powers regard the completion of their revolution
to be an essential preliminary to lasting peace, and nations
attempting to check it are the real aggressors; science has
outlawed war by making it an instrument of universal destruction.

Now, without any elaborate discussion of the theory of
international relations, for which self-restraint one is grate-
ful, Mr. Eichelberger points out that the United Nations
can indeed face the grave issues confronting it, without a

xi

remaking of its Charter. By political action, rather than by legal formula, the members of the United Nations can make the Charter work, so as to furnish a shield against that final anarchy of nations which would resort to the use of the supreme last weapon, hydrogen or cobalt bomb. The strengthening of the strategy of peace, which has been the constant aim of the United Nations, including technical and other assistance and international co-operation in such plans as "Atoms for Peace," is the way out of the cold war or the threat of other wars.

Mr. Eichelberger's thesis of the future of the United Nations is based on a close study of its history. As one of the little committee of the State Department which drew the blueprint of the Charter and then as Director of the American Association for the United Nations, he writes with authority, firm in his conviction as to fundamentals, yet with an open mind as to the subordinate details. The pattern is already fixed, its completion is all that is called for.

JAMES T. SHOTWELL

UN: The First Ten Years

CHAPTER I

Introduction

The United Nations is on the eve of its tenth birthday. The framers of the Charter anticipated that the tenth year might provide an opportunity for a review of how well the organization has functioned.

They could not have anticipated how tremendous would be the stresses and strains to which the United Nations would be subjected in its first decade. Indeed, in that brief time the world has experienced scientific, political and social changes that stamp it as one of the most revolutionary decades in history.

These changes can best be described by considering four great developments which have taken place since the Charter was drafted in 1945. It is against these particularly that the achievements of the United Nations must be measured.

These four developments might be described as the breakup of the five-power system, the advent of the atomic age, the rapid liquidation of the colonial system and the revolt against misery by the underprivileged half of mankind.

It is a sufficient tribute to the United Nations to say that it has survived these changes. It is an even greater tribute to say that the United Nations has helped the world to survive these changes. Indeed, without the unifying moral force of the United Nations the world might not have been able to survive them.

Breakup of the five-power system

The late Secretary of State Stettinius, in presenting the
United Nations Charter to the Senate in 1945, stated that
giving the great powers a veto in the Security Council was
simply recognizing the power facts of life. The United
Nations, he said, must depend for success upon the unanimity
of the five great powers. Others said that the world organization would be dependent for security on the five world
policemen, as they were called.

The five-power system has dissolved and the United Nations has survived. Russia quickly exiled herself from the
circle of great power unanimity by demanding that unanimity must always be on her terms. She has used the veto some
sixty times to enforce her will. The Chinese Nationalist Government is in exile. France is recovering slowly. Only Britain
and the United States are capable or willing to exercise the
particular responsibilities imposed upon them by the Charter
as great powers on the Security Council.

It was a mistake to assume that five great powers under
any circumstances could remain united for a decade. It was
equally a mistake to believe that the five great powers of
1945 would necessarily be the five great powers of 1955.

The United Nations in 1950 recognized this change in the
world's power situation. The Assembly adjusted the organization to the new power situation by shifting the center of
gravity from the Security Council to the General Assembly
where the veto does not prevail. This was accomplished
through the Uniting for Peace Resolution adopted to prevent a Soviet veto from blocking further action to defeat
aggression in Korea.

Advent of the atomic age

The closing days of the San Francisco Conference, in
retrospect, present a weird picture. The statesmen did not

know that soon after they were to adjourn an atomic bomb
would be dropped which would profoundly change the security calculations upon which the Charter was based. Secretary
Dulles, one of the drafters, has stated that had they known
that an atomic bomb was shortly to be dropped, they would
have made the Charter a stronger document with authority
for the control of weapons of mass destruction. Be that as it
may, the advent of weapons of mass destruction, first atomic
and then hydrogen bombs, had a profound effect upon the
world whose peace the United Nations was to safeguard.

Breakup of the colonial system

One fourth of mankind, six hundred million people, has
won its independence since the war ended. The remaining two
hundred million non-self governing peoples are demanding
their freedom.

It is doubtful that the rapidity of this development was
anticipated at San Francisco. However, the eventual doom
of the colonial system was foreshadowed in a number of liberal provisions of the Charter. In the spirit of sacrifice that
sometimes comes to peoples under the strain of war, certain
governments promised their dependencies freedom if they
and the mother countries were liberated. The Queen of the
Netherlands promised self-government to the people of
Indonesia—a promise which, unfortunately, was not honored
easily after the war.

Important ones of these liberated nations have taken their
place in the United Nations. Others, such as Libya and the
three states of Indo-China, have applied but have not yet
been admitted. Indeed, statesmen from the major liberated
areas, have provided the United Nations with some of its
leadership. The United Nations has provided an opportunity for newly freed people to adjust themselves to the
family of nations. It has provided a place where people could

petition for their freedom. It has provided a safety valve.
Without the orderly process which the United Nations provided, this revolutionary factor of six hundred million people
clamoring for independence might well have upset the world
with its violence and thus given communism its greatest
opportunity.

Revolt against misery

The revolt against political colonialism has been accompanied by a revolt against economic colonialism. Miserable people over large areas of the world are aware that somewhere
people are less miserable. They want to improve their lives.
They are growing increasingly restless. As a response to
this desire there is a program of world helpfulness to help
people help themselves. It is called by the uninspiring phrase
"technical assistance." It has been carried forward by the
United States Point Four Program and the Colombo plan.
However, the project has reached its broadest development
in the United Nations where some seventy political units,
more than its membership, have begun a program that makes
possible joint responsibility between the privileged and the
underprivileged and thus even makes it possible for the
underprivileged to help each other.

These four developments are basic in any measurement
of the achievements of the United Nations in its first decade.
Obviously other factors must be taken into consideration,
such as the idealism and selfishness of governments.

In this analysis it will be shown that the United Nations
of 1955 is quite different from the United Nations of 1945.
The organization has grown in unanticipated ways.

Moral unity

An assessment of the value of the United Nations must

take into account the fact that the organization has stood as the symbol of moral unity. This was necessary to keep the peace. This contribution is greater than any specific settlement it has made and transcends its failures.

Suppose the nations had entered the atomic age in a world of anarchy, had not under the leadership of the late President Roosevelt resolved, while fighting, to write the charter? What if they had not crystallized this intention in the formally adopted principles of good conduct with laws against war? Suppose the nations had not created a common meeting place with machinery for the peaceful settlement of disputes, or for enabling men to develop in larger freedom! It is doubtful that the world would have survived this long. The disruptive potentialities of the changes in the immediate postwar period were so great and their capacity for destruction so terrible that without the unifying moral force of the United Nations the world might have destroyed itself.

Sixty nations are at least legally bound by all of the obligations of the Charter. Several more are bound by one or more of its articles. An additional twenty-one have asked to be admitted to these obligations. The Charter provides that all nations, irrespective of membership, shall " . . . act in accordance with these Principles so far as may be necessary for the maintenance of international peace and security." An even greater number of nations belong to various specialized agencies.

A large proportion of the members of the United Nations have displayed a striking similarity of view in their votes on many of the issues before the General Assembly. Even the five Soviet and satellite states, who usually vote against the overwhelming majority, attempt to justify their conduct on the basis of the obligations of the Charter.

How does one describe this intangible quality of moral and spiritual unity as represented by the United Nations? Sometimes it is discernible in the political field, as when fifty-three nations supported the second Security Council resolution of June 27, 1950, on Korea. Or when the General Assembly overwhelmingly passed the Uniting for Peace Resolution, which recognized that in that body rested the strength of the organization. Sometimes this quality is displayed in the human rights field, as when the General Assembly with but eight abstentions adopted the Universal Declaration of Human Rights. One catches its spirit when some seventy nations pledge themselves to contribute amounts, some large and some small, to the United Nations Technical Assistance Fund. Sometimes it is revealed in the area dealing with dependent peoples when representatives of a large part of mankind must listen to an African native plead for self-government for his people under the provisions of the Charter.

Reflections of this spirit of unity can be found in strange places. Military men borrowed from different countries are stationed at mountain passes in Kashmir; others are supervising mixed commissions in Palestine. Modern missionaries on technical assistance missions can be found in some forty countries helping people grow better crops, check illness and establish education. All of these are practical manifestations of an intangible spirit which has held the world together so far.

The first obligation of any people and any government and any statesman is continuously to contribute to this sense of world unity for which the United Nations provides both the framework of principles and the machinery for action. Any people, any government or any statesman who unconsciously, thoughtlessly or deliberately detracts from or weakens this sense of unity is damaging the fabric of peace and contributing to a third world war.

The greatest danger that the peace of the world faces today is that the nations lose the vision of this moral unity and bypass the common meeting place of the United Nations. The greatest danger is that growing tired of the effort to think and act in world terms they may try to fragmentize their concerns in local settlements. This warning is not against regional political, economic and spiritual understanding as such; but rather against any that are not thought of as contributing to the over-all system of world order. The problems of the world are one. And if this vision is lost, the world is lost.

CHAPTER II

Peaceful Adjustment and Settlement

The purpose of the United Nations is the maintenance of peace. For this the Charter provides varying methods. One is the development of a dynamic international society in which nations are held together by many visible and intangible bonds of civilized adjustment. Another is the more obvious, the settlement of disputes and the promotion of disarmament. And finally, when violence breaks out, the United Nations provides the means for arresting aggression.

The entire United Nations and its specialized agencies are dedicated to the development of a dynamic international society. Means for the settlement of disputes are to be found in Chapter VI of the Charter, supplemented by the peaceful procedures of the General Assembly, as provided for in Chapter IV.

Authorization for the prevention of aggression is to be found in Chapter VII of the Charter and in general articles dealing with the Security Council and the General Assembly. This chapter concerns itself primarily with controversies and disputes, leaving the subject of collective security to stop aggression to the next chapter.

The Charter itself recognizes a series of graduated situations progressing from "questions" and "matters," to "situations" and "disputes."

The United Nations provides an atmosphere and means

for adjustment. These means may be of various kinds—debates in the General Assembly, informal conferences in the Delegates' Lounge or inspection teams on United Nations missions. In various technological conferences scientists, psychologists, doctors and farmers meet. There is a constant multiplicity of contacts in many areas of human living which sets the climate and method of adjustment, and provides an atmosphere of permanence. Hundreds of regular and *ad hoc* meetings take place annually. Exaggerated diplomatic protocol is absent. The presumption is that the meetings will advance peace. Hence each meeting is impelled by the cumulative effect of previous meetings going on and new ones to come. The results of each conference must be reported to the central body.

Here might be a good place to consider the fallacious or outmoded argument that peace and adjustment cannot be made in a goldfish bowl. Secret diplomacy is often erroneously presented as an alternative to the newly tried technique of public discussion. Since today's problems are increasingly world-wide, and whatever two or three nations do may very well affect the lives of all peoples, most nations are concerned with everything that goes on in the world. They will not be content with old-fashioned, secret, bilateral diplomacy which excludes them.

This is not to say that many times private negotiations are not to be preferred to the passion of public debate. Repeatedly the General Assembly has urged the great powers to get together in private discussions to clear the way for larger agreements, particularly in the field of disarmament. The representatives of the United States and the U.S.S.R. in private discussions could agree to the lifting of the Berlin blockade after a public hearing of the issue had reached no conclusion. But the two ambassadors met part of the time within the physical confines and always within the moral confines of the United Nations. Private discussions conducted within the premises of the United Nations or under its purposes and principles are very different from the private discussions of nineteenth-century diplomacy.

William Frye of the *Christian Science Monitor*, in a working paper for the Fifth American Assembly in 1954, well summarized some of the values of public meetings: they mobilize public opinion; they serve to restrain extremists; they serve the purpose of putting agreements "on the record"; they often hasten the process of private negotiation by setting a deadline for settlement; and sometimes they afford an opportunity to blow off steam. And we should add, they lead to many adjustments.

Sometimes the process of adjustment and debate is not enough. A dispute may then be presented to the Security Council under Chapter VI of the Charter as likely to endanger international peace and security. It may also go to the General Assembly. The Charter prefers normal diplomacy first. The parties to any dispute " . . . the continuance of which is likely to endanger the maintenance of international peace and security, shall, first of all, seek a solution by negotiation, enquiry, mediation, conciliation, arbitration, judicial settlement, resort to regional agencies or arrangements, or other peaceful means of their own choice." But back of this wide variety is presumed to be the firm hand of the Security Council backed by Chapter VI and the moral authority of the General Assembly.

A wide variety of disputes have been before the United Nations. Secretary-General Trygve Lie, in his report to the Fourth Assembly, said: "United Nations action in other parts of the world has also contributed to the progress made towards a more peaceful world by either preventing or ending wars involving five hundred million people." The United Nations has acted with much flexibility, imagination and courage in dealing with disputes. It has developed methods and techniques which, although not spelled out in the Charter, have their authority in articles outlining the competence of the Security Council and the General Assembly. For illustration, the Security Council or the General Assembly has appointed commissions to watch troubled frontiers such as the Greek border and the Thirty-eighth Parallel in Korea. Both steps resulted from a liberal interpretation of the right of both bodies to establish "such subsidiary organs as it deems necessary for the performance of its functions," plus the fact that the General Assembly can initiate studies and the Security Council may investigate any troublesome dispute or situation.

Another illustration is the Secretary-General's use of his authority in Article 97 giving him the right to have such staff as necessary to perform his duties. At one time because of necessity and by means of bold improvisation, the Secretary-General had a force of seven hundred guards, radio technicians, chauffeurs, automobile mechanics and others, accompanying United Nations missions in the field. Such a force might well be the beginning of a United Nations Legion.

The Security Council has successfully used the process of mediation. A committee of three governments negotiated the truce and formulated the principles of the Renville Agreement. This made possible the Round Table Conference at The Hague which resulted in Indonesia winning her independence and becoming a member of the United Nations. Dr. Frank Graham, in drafting the Renville Agreement, is credited with a major success in this endeavor. The late Count Folke Bernadotte, one of the first United Nations martyrs, and Dr. Ralph Bunche, one of the ablest of UN mediators, provided a most dramatic illustration of mediation by persuading Israel and the Arab states to sign armistice agreements and to set up mixed commissions to enforce them.

In both cases there were two important factors: the excellence of the mediators and the support of the United Nations.

In Kashmir, where there was fierce fighting between the forces of India and Pakistan, a United Nations Commission of five helped to work out a cease-fire and an agreement for a plebiscite. Since then a series of mediators have been attempting to clear the way for the plebiscite.

One of the most successful methods which the United Nations has used to maintain peace is dispatching on-the-spot commissions to observe threats to frontiers. Such a commission stationed on Greece's frontier may have been one of the most important factors in deterring invasion from Greece's Communist neighbors. When Yugoslavia broke from the Cominform in 1948 and made peace with Greece, the commission was withdrawn. The method, however, was considered so successful that a Peace Observation Commission for the Balkans was substituted.

The United Nations commissions are of various compositions and serve in many different situations. Military men borrowed from various countries are in Kashmir guarding mountain passes to prevent a clash between the armed forces of India and Pakistan. The mixed commissions stationed on the frontiers of Israel and the Arab states provide a basis for the belligerents coming together. *Ad hoc* committees deal with such practical problems as authorizing the possession of a water hole, returning cattle who do not know frontiers, and assessing the blame for armed bands marauding on the other side of the line. A United Nations Commission at the Thirty-eighth Parallel in Korea was able to certify to the facts of aggression within a few hours on June 25, 1950. Commissions of inquiry studied the situation in Italian

Somaliland and Eritrea to guide the United Nations in the determination of their future.

The Security Council, as the organ primarily responsible for the maintenance of international peace and security, is placed in the Charter virtually on a level with the General Assembly. As previously described, the Security Council was intended to represent the power facts of life. The five great powers, the U.S.A., the United Kingdom, France, U.S.S.R. and the Republic of China, have permanent seats on the Security Council. The remaining six non-permanent seats are rotated. In selecting the non-permanent members, the General Assembly was to give consideration to the contributions they could make to peace and security and to the other purposes of the organization, as well as to geographical distribution.

Affirmative decisions on substantive matters were to be taken by a majority of seven, providing that the seven included the affirmative votes of the great powers. By tacit agreement an abstention is not considered a veto. But it is this requirement of great power unanimity that has weakened the importance of the Security Council and enhanced the General Assembly.

The Security Council, in the absence of the Soviet Union, reached its highest point of effectiveness when it passed two resolutions authorizing resistance to aggression in Korea. Beginning with its mobilization of public opinion to force the withdrawal of Soviet troops from Iran in 1946, through its two decisions regarding aggression in Korea in June, 1950, the Security Council has a record of important and valuable work. Wherever the chilling effect of the cold war was absent the Security Council could function as it was intended to. But as the spread of the cold war has extended to one geographical area after another, the Security Council has been reduced in influence. The cold war has now reached the Middle East, and so even in disputes involving Israel and her Arab neighbors the Soviet veto is now cast.

An examination of the meetings which the Security Council has held year by year is indicative of its decline. This body is set up technically to be in continuous session. Its rules of procedure call for a meeting every two weeks. Nevertheless, the number of Security Council meetings during the first nine years is: 1946—88; 1947—137; 1948—168; 1949—62; 1950—73; 1951—39; 1952—42; 1953—42; 1954—32. When it is recognized that some of these meetings were routine to adopt reports, the situation seems even more serious.

The paralysis of the Security Council is due first of all to the Soviet veto. Its veto has now been cast some sixty times. If the Soviet Union had deliberately determined to reduce the importance of the Security Council upon which it presumes to pin so much hope, it could not have been more effective. Even from the standpoint of Soviet policy, some of these vetoes seem beyond reason.

In the second place the nations of the West tend to think of most problems in terms of the containment of communism. Granting that this is a logical reaction to Soviet policy, the fact remains that the powers on the Security Council exhibit less objectivity in facing disputes.

If one reviews the issues which the Security Council has resolved peaceably, one is reluctantly forced to the conclusion that if these issues were before the Security Council today they might not be similarly resolved for two reasons: First, the Soviet Union, having banished any area in which it could act objectively, would cast a veto for its own purposes. Second, it is to be feared that the United States, the United Kingdom and France, reacting to Soviet policies, might subordinate United Nations principles to cold war strategy.

It has become increasingly difficult to give adequate representation to all sections of the world, particularly to Asia, in the Security Council. With only six seats to be rotated and with the division fairly stereotyped regionally, some areas of the world have reason to feel that they are not adequately represented.

Mr. Nehru well pointed out that the Security Council, as elected by the Eighth General Assembly, contained no real representation for half of the population of the world that lives in Asia. Over a billion people in that area were presumed to be represented by New Zealand and Lebanon. The population of the first country is not considered Asiatic, and Lebanon is Middle Eastern.

It has been said that the decline of the Security Council as the United Nations principal peacemaking organ and the emergence of the General Assembly is unquestionably the most significant constitutional development which has taken place in the United Nations.

The General Assembly has now become the paramount organ of adjustment. It provides a forum for the airing of grievances and injustices and exposing potentially dangerous situations. Here there is no way in which any nation can block discussion. The provisions for inserting items on its agenda are in themselves liberal. Furthermore, the general debate on the Report of the Secretary-General provides an opportunity to discuss almost any subject. Nor is debate limited by what a particular nation may consider its domestic concern—the General Assembly, being the judge of its own competence, has discussed the Union of South Africa's treatment of its Indian minority or its mandate for Southwest Africa. Here, somehow, the voice of a suppressed people may find expression through a champion.

The debate in the General Assembly is a good gauge of the climate of world public opinion. It is a thermometer for measuring the temperature of the cold war. After several months of discussion in this forum any major power can find out whether its views, hammered out in debate and private discussion, represent those of a considerable number of member states.

There were some at San Francisco, including the author, who predicted that within a very short period of time the General Assembly would become the paramount body of the United Nations. Even if the Security Council had not become partially paralyzed, this would have occurred, although at a slower pace, because the General Assembly is its most democratic body, representing all states.

The General Assembly has increasingly become a means for dealing with disputes. It has provided for elections in Korea, stationed a commission on the Thirty-eighth Parallel and one on the Greek frontier after the Security Council refused to renew its original commission. The Assembly at its Ninth Session decided to request the Secretary-General to carry out the Assembly resolution calling for the return of American and other prisoners of war held by the Chinese Communists in violation of the armistice agreements.

However, it was the fortunes of war in Korea that led to the Uniting for Peace Resolution which clearly outlined the competence of the General Assembly to act against aggression. This resolution, while recognizing that the Security Council was primarily responsible for the maintenance of international peace and security, clearly recognized the authority of the Assembly to act if the Security Council was blocked by the veto. The Assembly revised its rules of procedure to provide for extraordinary sessions within twenty-four hours, rather than fourteen days as previously provided.

What procedures, short of revision of the Charter, could be recommended for a development in United Nations peace-making machinery?

The statesmen must proceed on both of two assumptions: The first is that the Security Council will continue to be paralyzed by the Soviet Union and the cold war, and consequently the General Assembly must increasingly carry the burden of peaceful settlement. The other is that the Security Council will be restored, at least partially, to its original effectiveness.

Assuming that the General Assembly is to take over the burden of peacemaking, it must develop procedures and possibly permanent organs to supplement its present methods. As matters now stand, it has or shares a number of bodies. The Trusteeship Council and the Economic and Social Council report to it. The Peace Observation Commission, established by the Uniting for Peace Resolution, can be used by the Security Council or the General Assembly if one of the member states requests such an observation commission. The Disarmament Commission, composed of members of the Security Council plus Canada, is responsible both to the General Assembly and the Security Council. The Collective Measures Committee was created by the General Assembly under the Uniting for Peace Resolution and reports to it.

However, something more may be needed. The General Assembly may be faced with the necessity of remaining in continuous session, having its First Committee remain in continuous session, or providing for subcommittees to deal with specific disputes it might assign to it.

The General Assembly is confronted with the following dilemma. If its sessions are too long, responsible statesmen cannot attend an adequate number of meetings. If there are serious problems before it, such as Korea, it may recess instead of adjourning, as in the case of the Seventh and Eighth Assemblies, but without continuing peacemaking machinery to function in its absence.

As an example, the Seventh Assembly, when it reconvened

in August, 1953, gave the Government of the United States
the responsibility of getting the "two sides" together for a
conference to unify Korea. It then recessed without leaving
any continuing machinery to function in the interim. The
result was that it temporarily relinquished control of the
peacemaking phase of the Korea issue. Taking advantage of
this situation the Soviet Union confronted the United States,
United Kingdom and France with a request for a Geneva
Conference outside of the United Nations. The results are
well known.

There are several procedures which the General Assembly
could employ better to fulfill its peacemaking role. Its First
Committee, dealing with political problems, could remain in
continuous session. It might divide itself into subcommittees
to attempt to mediate, investigate and suggest peaceful settlements. But to be effective in the interim between regular
Assembly sessions, it must have the powers of the General
Assembly. The experience of the "Little Assembly" must
be avoided. That body failed because it could only do
what the General Assembly charged it to do and the Soviet
Union refused to recognize it.

Another procedure might be for the General Assembly to
set up *ad hoc* committees to deal with particular disputes
between sessions, such as that between Israel and the Arab
states.

The Uniting for Peace Resolution changed the rules of
procedure so that the General Assembly could meet within
twenty-four hours instead of fourteen days in case it had to
act against aggression because the Security Council was
paralyzed, presumably by the veto. A similar resolution
could be adopted by the General Assembly to deal with disputes.

The United Nations may be on the eve of very important
steps such as the peacetime use of atomic energy and the

inspection and control to accompany disarmament. These will necessitate important organs of authority and control. As the world develops, other organs will be added. They must be attached somewhere; the only central body to which they can be attached effectively would seem to be the General Assembly, which is composed of all the members. Consequently, if the United Nations is to grow, the Assembly must grow.

The increased authority and responsibility which the trend of events has given the General Assembly impose on that body and the statesmen who attend considerable self-discipline and maturity. The leading statesmen of the world must spend a greater amount of time in attendance, no matter how difficult this may be for them. Without gag rule and without shutting off debate, the Assembly must find a way of conducting its business with even greater dispatch so that responsible statesmen can participate in the major part of the deliberations. The statesmen must voluntarily put a curb on themselves as far as bloc voting, log-rolling and selfish ambition are concerned.

Probably the most specific recommendation that could be made here is that the General Assembly set up a commission to study how its procedures may be developed in the light of increasing responsibilities.

The balance between the Security Council and the General Assembly which the architects of San Francisco thought they had created in the Charter is not likely to be restored. The Assembly will almost certainly continue to be the paramount body of the organization. However, the Security Council might be restored as an important body responsible for dealing with disputes if the great powers, particularly the Soviet Union, demonstrate two qualities. The first is the ability to move from fixed positions to conciliation. The second is the capacity of their Council representatives to think of themselves not merely as delegates from their respective countries, but as representatives of the world as a whole.

What is the most dramatic way in which the importance of the Security Council could be to a certain extent revived? It might be time to take advantage of an unused article in the Charter. Article 28 provides for holding periodic meetings of the Security Council which the heads of state would attend. Trygve Lie urged such a meeting several years ago. From time to time during Assembly debates various states have suggested calling such a meeting. For some time it has been suggested that there be a meeting of the Big Four. In this critical moment, both in Europe and the Far East, an extraordinary Security Council meeting could be called which heads of state, including the Big Four, would attend for an over-all review of the world situation.

There are improvements in procedures for investigation, etc., of which either the General Assembly or the Security Council could take advantage. More liberal use of the Peace Observation Commission could be made, sending teams to many troubled frontiers such as that of Thailand and Indo-China or to cover the whole Indo-Chinese area to see that the Geneva settlement is being observed. A Peace Observation Commission could well be dispatched to the Formosa Strait. Such commissions could be given wide latitude to mediate as well as to observe. The Peace Observation Commission should have authority to act on its own initiative, or at the request of a member state, without waiting for authorization from the General Assembly or the Security Council.

Again, the problem goes back to the governments and the people. For the first seven years the United Nations used resourcefulness in finding approaches to the peaceful settlement of disputes. The peoples and their governments willed it. The pressure of public opinion was so strong and the techniques so ably carried out that few could resist. In the past two years the peacemaking process has tended to become stalemated. The plebiscite has not been held in Kashmir. The Israeli-Arab armistice agreements have not been translated into permanent peace treaties. The United Nations was by-passed in the Trieste settlement. Indo-China is a tragic monument to the unwillingness of statesmen to present a problem to the United Nations while there was still time for a settlement that could have averted much tragedy and sacrifice.

All states, particularly the great powers, must continue and increase the habit of conciliation through the United Nations. The conciliation procedures of the United States are many. Blocked in one approach the nations should try another. Neither secret diplomacy nor the Geneva type conference outside of the United Nations will fundamentally reduce the tensions that confront the nations. All states must put the cause of peace, justice and conciliation ahead of ideological differences and selfish concerns.

CHAPTER III

Collective Security

United Nations resistance to aggression at the Thirty-eighth Parallel in Korea, undertaken on the initiative of the United States, is history's most nearly complete example of collective security. It was authorized organized action on the part of many nations to stop aggression in violation of the principles of the world organization. This resistance brought the United Nations to a high point of unity and achievement. It was also accompanied by the tragic disappointments to be expected in any great and new endeavor.

Resistance to aggression in Korea had almost all of the elements that should be associated with collective security. First, the fact of aggression was certified to by an agency of the United Nations. This certification was so complete that when the Security Council met on June 25, 1950, to consider the aggression, no nation dared ask for a delay on the excuse that the facts were not known. This is a far cry from 1932 when the nations dispatched a commission under the direction of Lord Lytton to Manchuria to secure the facts. By the time this commission had traveled to the Pacific area by train and by boat and formulated its condemnation of Japan, the Japanese had Manchuria.

Furthermore, resistance to aggression was authorized step by step by the legally constituted bodies of the United Nations. The basic resolutions placing the United Nations against aggression were passed by the Security Council in the absence of the Soviet Union. Later the General Assembly took over the direction of events in Korea.

Another attribute of collective security was fulfilled by the Korean action in that the burden of resistance to aggression was shared at least in some degree by a large number of nations. Sixteen members of the United Nations sent fighting forces. Several members sent heroic hospital units. Additional contingents could have been had. Almost forty nations sent material aid of some kind.

And, finally, there was a United Nations Command. The Security Council asked the President of the United States to name a supreme commander under whose authority the national contingents would fight.

It is true that there have been other examples of collective security where nations co-operated under a supreme commander to resist aggression, as in the case of allied resistance to German aggression in the First and Second World Wars. However, allied resistance was never authorized by an established body of the world community. Indeed, had the League of Nations authorized resistance to aggression the day Germany attacked Poland, the League might well have been a moral force guiding the nations during the Second World War. It might then have gained new stature and the establishment of the United Nations to take its place would have been unnecessary.

It seems important to devote some attention to how collective security operated in the Korean affair because it gives us lessons for the future.

Korea gave the world hope that the nations could take collective action; if not against a great power, certainly against a satellite of a great power. It also demonstrated that resistance would continue if a great power entered the struggle. At San Francisco it was stated that since the success of the United Nations would depend upon the unity of the great powers, the organization could not take action against any one of them. Consequently, it was against the aggressions of smaller states that the Charter was directed. This seemed worth while because many times the disputes of smaller states lead to the conflict of the great. However, when the test came, the United Nations did proceed against the wishes of the Soviet Union and resisted the armed intervention of the Chinese Communist Government.

No one could have been more surprised than the Russians at the United Nations action on June 25, 1950. The Soviet Government was guilty of one of its frequent miscalculations when, not believing that the members of the Security Council would do anything to deter aggression in Korea, it continued its boycott of the Security Council.

It can now be revealed that discussion had gone on among some of the members of the Security Council to consider whether, if the Soviet representative cast a veto, they would call a special session of the General Assembly. While technically the Assembly's rules of procedure provide for a period of fourteen days before its convening, the statesmen might well have agreed to overlook this technicality.

There was boldness in 1950. With breathtaking speed the UN found a way to circumvent the veto in what amounted to a revolution. In November, 1950, after the Soviet Union had returned to the Security Council, the General Assembly adopted the Uniting for Peace Resolution and shifted the center of gravity from the Security Council to itself. The Security Council had proved itself incapable of expressing the power situation of the world that had come to exist. Consequently the General Assembly adjusted the United Nations more nearly to the realities of the new power situation.

The results of the action against aggression in Korea were felt in many directions. A projected train of aggression may have been interrupted and a third world war avoided. Western Europe, particularly, took heart because aggression could be met and stopped. The Atlantic community took on additional vitality and the NATO army developed.

On the other hand, this first effort of United Nations resistance to aggression revealed certain weaknesses both in the co-operation of the member states and in the machinery and the procedures of collective security. There was an unevenness in the determination of governments to fulfill their Charter obligations. The collective security machinery of the United Nations was not complete when Korean aggression occurred. Consequently there were balks and mistakes which robbed the victory of collective security of even greater brightness.

The United Nations had no forces at its command to weld into an international army. The nations had not complied with Article 43 of the Charter to designate forces for use by the Security Council. Consequently the United States, because it had forces closest at hand, was called upon to make a disproportionate contribution of men and matériel. The acceptance of contingents and building them into a truly international army were a matter of improvisation.

The United Nations lacked a general staff that might have appointed a supreme commander and assessed the political consequences of his acts in the field. The Military Staff Committee provided for in the Charter was unworkable both because the Soviet Union was a member of it and because it did not bear adequate relationship to the nations that had fighting forces in Korea. As an alternative, the above nations developed an *ad hoc* basis for co-ordination of military efforts. The diplomatic representatives of these nations met regularly at the State Department in Washington. Consequently the collective action was more and more directed by Washington rather than by the United Nations. Some of the nations were altogether too willing to leave the conduct of

military operations with accompanying praise and blame
to the United States. And American military men were quite
willing to accept this responsibility.

Somewhere in this evolving situation there occurred the
march to the Yalu River. This event is still an untouchable in American public discussion.

On October 21, 1950, the Supreme Commander could
report to the United Nations that the tide of battle had
turned and that the backbone of the North Korean Army
was broken; on November 3 operations were in progress to
destroy all North Korean forces. On October 7 the General
Assembly had passed a resolution which was ambiguously
worded to the extent that the United Nations Command
could interpret it as giving it authority to occupy all of
North Korea to unify the country.

One delegate in the Assembly Hall warned against this
northward march. The late Sir Benegal Rau of India told
the Assembly that his government had information that, if
such a course were pursued, the area of conflict might be
extended.

In retrospect Sir Benegal Rau's advice should have been
heeded. Had the Chinese Communists come in anyway, the
United Nations forces would have had a more defensible line
at the waist north of the Thirty-eighth Parallel. Possibly
they would not have come in. A great victory was turned into
a defeat. It took months for the United Nations forces to
fight their way back to the Thirty-eighth Parallel.

There was confusion in the United Nations at the moment
of victory as to the time and the method of negotiation. It is
a hard lesson for military men to learn that unconditional
surrender is not necessary for successful collective security.
When aggression is stopped, peaceful negotiations should be
under way. It is not necessary to destroy the aggressor.

In retrospect, the United Nations should have been at-

tempting negotiations for peaceful settlement while resistance was going on. In fact confidential diplomatic talks had
been going on to secure a neutral zone along the Yalu River
but military events rendered them futile. Indeed, Chapter
VII of the Charter, providing for United Nations action
against the aggressor, might well have been followed by
another chapter outlining simultaneous procedures for negotiations with the aggressor as he is being driven back.

Neither was the United Nations prepared for peacemaking in Korea upon the signing of an armistice and cease-fire.
When the Seventh Assembly met in recessed session in August, 1953, to set up a political conference, it was anticipated
that most of the members of the United Nations would have
a sense of achievement that aggression had been defeated by
the collective will of mankind. A new list of martyrs was
added to those who had struggled for freedom—the United
Nations armed forces.

However, to everyone's consternation there was disagree-
ment as to who should represent the United Nations at the
conference. Was it to be a round table conference or a conference of "two sides." The focal point of the argument was
India. It was the wish of over half of the members of the
United Nations, but not two-thirds, that India should be
on the delegation. The United States opposed India's participation, partly because of President Syngman Rhee's
violent objection.

The United States position weakened the concept of collective security at the moment of victory. It argued that
only those who had fighting forces in Korea were entitled to
sit at the political conference and that other members were
in effect neutrals. This concept did not give sufficient recognition to the fact that the United Nations collectively had
resisted aggression, that forty-four had voted Communist

China an aggressor, and that almost forty members had supplied material aid.

Resistance to aggression in Korea is one of the most important steps in the development of the United Nations. It marked a new point in history, for many nations demonstrated that collectively they could and would resist aggression. At the same time many lessons are to be learned from the United Nations first effort of this kind.

The Uniting for Peace Resolution established a Collective Measures Committee for the study of improvements in procedures for collective security. Unfortunately it has not met frequently in recent years. Indeed, the nations seem to hesitate to talk about universal collective security because of the lack of a clear-cut end to the Korean problem and because of their preoccupation with regional arrangements. However, this Committee did make a report to the Ninth General Assembly which contained some constructive suggestions and the Assembly continued it on a stand-by basis.

The first step in strengthening procedures for future resistance to aggression should be to strengthen this Committee and put it on a full-time basis.

Certain recommendations, some emanating from this Committee, should be pushed. The members of the United Nations immediately should designate forces for use by the Security Council under Article 43 of the Charter or for use of the General Assembly under the Uniting for Peace Resolution. As is more fully outlined in the chapter on regional arrangements, forces designated by member states for use by regional systems should be designated for use by the United Nations.

Provisions for joint financing of contingents from countries unable to pay and train them should be worked out now. Ambassador Lodge is the authority for the statement that the United Nations could have had more troops in the field in Korea had it been willing to provide for their training and equipment when necessary.

A new military staff committee should be provided for. It must be sufficiently flexible to represent at any time those nations contributing troops or facilities to United Nations resistance to aggression. It should be able to appoint the Supreme Commander and assess the political consequences of his military acts in the field. It should serve either the Security Council or the General Assembly, whichever body authorizes resistance to aggression.

The United Nations should follow the suggestion of the Government of the United States and study the feasibility of a United Nations Legion. It should go further and establish this Legion.

This Legion, made up of men enlisting directly and wearing the uniform of the United Nations, could be rushed to any scene of potential or actual fighting. In most cases its presence might be sufficient to maintain or re-establish peace. Few nations would dare fire upon a United Nations army composed of young men who have enlisted from practically all of the United Nations member states. Any aggressor attacking such a force would not only be firing upon the collective symbol of the world community, but he would be firing upon citizens of practically every nation.

If, however, the presence of the United Nations Legion is not sufficiently strong in a moral or military sense to restrain the aggressor, then the contingents of member states could be rushed to the scene. But in many cases the presence of the Legion might be adequate.

The nations should consider other contributions beside the contingents and facilities to be made available to the collective security system. The question of strategic bases is a factor at this point. An effort is being made to bring con-

ventional weapons and weapons of mass destruction under a
system of law and order. However, less is said about strategic
bases than any other phase of the arms problem.

The search for strategic bases goes on feverishly. Its reac-
tions are felt in many quarters. American newspapers frequently print maps of the Northern Hemisphere showing
how well the United States is ringing the Soviet Union with
strategic bases. And the same newspapers point out how
Soviet bases in the Far North constantly bring Soviet bomb-
ing planes in closer range of the United States.

The question of strategic bases is one of the most important and yet one of the least discussed in the problems of
collective security and disarmament. Indeed, it could be as
well discussed under this chapter dealing with collective security as in the following dealing with disarmament. Some
way should be found to bring these bases within a world-
wide system of collective security. They should no longer be
factors contributing to the world's insecurity. Now, quite
obviously the nations are not going to dismantle these bases,
nor are they going to turn them over to the United Nations
for international administration at the present time.

What arrangement then could be made so that they contribute to world unity instead of world anarchy? Possibly
each nation could declare that under the spirit of Article 43
of the Charter and the Uniting for Peace Resolution these
bases were " . . . armed forces, assistance, and facilities . . . "
maintained for use if not administration by the United Nations.

Possibly a pattern could be found in the administration of
the bases which the United States secured from the British in
return for the overaged destroyers during World War II.
The United States made it clear that the members of the
Pan American Union, now the Inter-American system, would
have access to these bases in co-operation with the United

States in any effort of collective security in the Western Hemisphere. Following this pattern the United States could declare, and challenge others to do the same, that its strategic bases exist for the maintenance of the system of collective security and that, without sacrificing essential control, these bases would be open to all nations participating in resistance to aggression under the authority of the United Nations.

But if the United Nations is successful in its procedures of peaceful settlement, collective action to stop aggression will not be necessary. And some of the subjects treated under peaceful procedures may have an intimate relationship to collective security. A commission on a troubled frontier may not only prevent aggression as it has seemed to have done in the case of Greece, but it can certify to the facts of aggression as it did at the Thirty-eighth Parallel in Korea.

The nations today are attempting to build collective security on a regional basis. Such efforts and their relationship to the over-all United Nations system are the subjects of the next chapter.

CHAPTER IV

Regional Arrangements

A prominent statesman remarked that the nations have moved to the establishment of a world organization without passing through the stage of regional arrangements. He wonders, therefore, whether the universal system can succeed.

Why confront the world with a choice between the two systems? A universal organization is necessary; regional arrangements can be important counterparts.

A tendency is now in evidence to develop collective security regionally. It becomes increasingly the position of the Government of the United States and other Western powers that so long as Russia maintains her recalcitrant position it would be easier to pinpoint collective security through such arrangements.

These regional arrangements may be of help to the over-all system of collective security as represented and developed by the United Nations; or they may harm it. They may add to world peace; or they may detract from world peace depending upon the purpose of their founders, their composition and their method of functioning. The way in which regional arrangements may help or hinder the over-all community depends not only on legal formula and text. It depends upon the good will and thoughtfulness of the statesmen.

Two articles of the Charter are specifically a source of regional arrangements: Articles 51 and 52. Article 51 recognizes the " . . . right of individual or collective self-defense if an armed attack occurs against a Member of the United Nations, until the Security Council has taken the measures necessary to maintain international peace and security." Such measures shall be reported to the Security Council and shall not affect in any way the authority and responsibility of the Security Council to act. Article 51 was projected by the United States delegation at San Francisco to provide an escape from the confines of the veto to permit the inter-American system to act in stopping aggression without waiting for the Security Council.

Now strictly speaking, Article 51 contains no provision for a permanent regional arrangement. And yet it was a perfectly logical development that regional arrangements be projected, such as the North Atlantic Treaty Organization, based upon it. Indeed, Article 51 provides one of the most interesting examples of Charter evolution. Not only because it is becoming the basis of regional arrangements which are not specifically provided for but because the article itself has furnished a way around the Security Council veto. It has become a basis of the shift in the center of gravity from the Security Council to the General Assembly —the most important development in United Nations evolution.

The use of Article 51 as a way around the Security Council veto was advocated from two different quarters. In 1946 it was put forward by the Commission to Study the Organization of Peace, research affiliate of the American Association for the United Nations. It was also put forward by Hamilton Fish Armstrong, editor of *Foreign Affairs*. These suggestions for the use of Article 51, however, did not propose exclusive regional arrangements. The Commission suggested as an alternative to NATO a general treaty open to ratification by any member of the United Nations pledging itself to earmark forces and to act upon the recommendation of the General Assembly, including three of the permanent members of the Security Council, to stop aggression.

Later the idea of such a treaty was incorporated in the Thomas-Douglas Resolution. This resolution proposed that Congress pledge its support to a "supplementary agreement under Article 51 of the Charter open to all members of the United Nations, by which the signatories agree, if the Security Council is prevented from fulfilling its duties, to come to the aid of the victim of attack if requested to do so by a two thirds vote of the General Assembly, including three of the permanent members of the Security Council . . . "

Under Article 52 the use of regional arrangements is specifically authorized. Such arrangements are given a degree of priority under the Charter as procedures for peaceful settlement. United Nations members of such agencies " . . . shall make every effort to achieve pacific settlement of local disputes through such regional arrangements . . . before referring them to the Security Council." Under Article 53 the Council shall encourage the development of pacific settlement of local disputes through regional arrangements " . . . either on the initiative of the states concerned or by reference from the Security Council." "The Security Council shall, where appropriate, utilize such regional arrangements or agencies for enforcement action under its authority." However, no enforcement action shall be taken under regional arrangements without authorization of the Security Council.

Roughly speaking, regional arrangements based upon Article 51 are organized primarily to resist aggression from outside the region. Regional arrangements based upon Article 52 are made essentially for the maintenance of peace and the adjustment of difficulties within the region, although they may have the former purpose as well.

The North Atlantic Treaty is based upon Article 51; collective self-defense. It has essentially one purpose—to resist aggression from the outside. Quite obviously the aggression contemplated was from Eastern Europe. Except for some phrases concerning economic and military co-operation, the North Atlantic Treaty sets up no machinery for adjusting difficulties and promoting co-operation among its members. However, it was unthinkable that these nations of Europe from whence the First and Second World Wars originated should have no machinery for the adjustment of their mutual problems. Consequently an elaborate machinery has developed through the Brussels Pact, the European Coal and Steel Community, the Organization for European Economic Co-operation, etc.

While the Rio Pact is based upon Article 51, the Charter of the Organization of American States declares, "Within the United Nations, the Organization of American States is a regional agency." It contains considerable machinery for the adjustment of difficulties and the maintenance of peace within a region. At the same time, it has as a purpose the repelling of outside aggression or foreign interference. The Monroe Doctrine was a unilateral declaration on the part of the Government of the United States to prevent outside penetration in the Western Hemisphere. The Monroe Doctrine and the Pan American system have evolved into the Organization of American States. The Monroe Doctrine has given way to a multilateral system under which the nations have organized for a dual purpose: to maintain peace within a region; to prevent outside interference.

Obviously a regional arrangement could exist for other than security purposes. A group of nations (India, Pakistan, Burma, Ceylon and Indonesia), called the Colombo powers, are united economically in the Colombo Plan. From this association a certain ideological point of view is developing. The Colombo powers are coming to have collective weight in the counsels of Asia. Except for Pakistan, they represent a neutral bloc of states between the "Communist" and free nations. These powers are in consultation with African and Middle Eastern states. The result may be to crystallize a so-called neutral block standing between the Western and Cominform systems.

Many regional groups of varying kinds exist. But only about five are of such nature as to make a contribution to the peace of the world by their contribution to collective security. Among these might be mentioned the Organization of American States, the North Atlantic Treaty Organization, the British Commonwealth of Nations, the new Turk-Greek-Yugoslav arrangement and the Southeast Asia Treaty Organization. The Soviet system of alliances is not a highly organized regional arrangement, but rather a system of criss-cross alliances in which the Soviet Union has a completely dominant and aggressive position. Also, by no stretch of the imagination could the Arab League be called a collective security arrangement contributing to the peace of the world. At present, it is essentially a loose federation directed against Israel.

What are the benefits and what are the dangers of collective security regional arrangements under modern conditions?

On the positive side, it is proper and natural for neighbors in any region to organize to meet their common problems. And the more that such nations can deal with their problems, the more there is lifted from the United Nations the burden of local difficulties, and thus the organization is freer to handle problems of world concern. And as far as outside aggression is concerned, members of the United Nations, if organized regionally to resist the threat of aggression, can pinpoint their opposition in a more effective manner.

Finally, under regional arrangements, nations may proceed without the obstructionism of the Soviet Union. It is no wonder that statesmen, frustrated by the repeated Soviet veto, look to regionalism as a short cut to collective security.

The dangers are equally clear. A regional arrangement might contain a number of powers whose combined strength would overshadow the world organization. This is the danger of NATO, whose membership and population, industrial output, commerce and colonial dependencies represent a disproportionate part of the world's strength.

The danger must always be reckoned with, and possibly in some circumstances it is unavoidable, that a regional arrangement will create another such arrangement in opposition. In such a situation the danger of war may increase. Will SEATO, whose members are primarily Western in location or thought, be matched by a Communist Pacific pact? Will those outside react to form an organization of "neutrals" determined not to be involved in either the Soviet or the Western collective systems?

It is not possible to conceive of the entire world covered by neat regional arrangements. Many of the troubles of the world with which the United Nations has had to deal have occurred in vacuums where such an arrangement is impossible. There was no regional organization to which the United States or South Korea could appeal when the aggressor crossed the Thirty-eighth Parallel. There is no regional arrangement to which Israel can appeal for justice in the Middle East. Indonesia, Kashmir and Iran were serious problems confronting the United Nations. They did not fall within any regional security pattern.

However, the trend for some time may well be in the direction of collective security regional arrangements. Indeed, the Commission to Study the Organization of Peace in its study entitled "Regional Arrangements for Security and the United Nations" concludes that political regional arrangements are needed until the operation of collective security under the United Nations becomes more adequate. The Commission warns against what it calls the bipolarization of the world. It says:

Since World War II the Soviet system, including the Soviet Union, its European satellites and China, has developed as an aggressive agency of Russian imperialism and communist expansion. To defend the free world, the United States, Canada, the United Kingdom and Western Europe have created the North Atlantic Treaty Organization, now joined by Greece and Turkey. These two gigantic systems have functioned relatively independently of the United Nations. The result of their rivalry and mutual fears has been an arms race tending to draw states to one side or the other, to weaken the United Nations as an agency of collective security, and to threaten a new world war.

The Commission believes that the United Nations and its members should seek to stop a trend toward a bipolarized world by fostering various centers of power and committing each to United Nations responsibilities.

What steps should be undertaken so that regional security arrangements are brought under the United Nations and thus contribute to world security? Indeed, it would seem to be time for the United Nations to adopt a code to govern the relationship of regional arrangements to it. It would be appropriate for the United States, as the foremost advocate of regional arrangements and the nation that is a party to many of them, to take the initiative in the General Assembly for proposing such a code.

In the first place, there should be minimum requirements for the relationship of regional security arrangements to the United Nations. A glance at those already created will show how strong or weak this relationship is at present. For illustration, the North Atlantic Treaty is based upon Article 51 of the Charter. The parties agree to halt military operations whenever the Security Council has taken necessary measures.

The Greek-Turk-Yugoslav agreement reaffirms loyalty to the United Nations Charter but does not refer to Article 51. However, the three nations agree that they will discontinue their three-power resistance in favor of the United Nations if the United Nations takes action. SEATO, however, while reaffirming the loyalty of its members to the United Nations, provides for no practical procedural co-operation.

The agreement signed on October 3, 1954, for the admission of Germany to the Brussels Pact and possibly into NATO introduced a new element. Here, an ex-enemy state and a non-member of the United Nations accepts not only the principles of the United Nations, but agrees specifically to accept the obligations of Article 2 of the Charter as a prerequisite for its joining NATO, the Brussels Pact, etc. It will be remembered that the obligations of Article 2 are very broad, including refraining from " . . . threat or use of force . . . " in its international relations; giving the United Nations "every assistance in any action it takes in accordance with the present Charter . . . "; and to settle its " . . . disputes by peaceful means . . . " etc.

The following are some of the points that might well be included in a code to govern the relationship of regional organizations to the United Nations:

1. There should be community judgment before or after the fact. If the build-up of aggression is sufficiently gradual, the Security Council or the General Assembly can authorize local and anticipate world-wide resistance. But if it is necessary for certain nations to act automatically under the provisions of Article 51, then the authorization of the Security Council or the General Assembly should be sought after the resistance to aggression takes place. Reports on collective defense in any regional arrangement under Articles 51 and

52 of the Charter should, in view of the Uniting for Peace Resolution, be transmitted to the General Assembly as well as to the Security Council.

2. Military forces contributed or designated for regional organizations should be considered military forces designated for use of the Security Council under Article 43 of the Charter or the General Assembly under the provisions of the Uniting for Peace Resolution.

The United Nations has not been successful in securing the implementation of Article 43 for the designation of military forces for the Security Council. Neither have forces been designated for implementing the Uniting for Peace Resolution. However, some nations, in response to a United Nations questionnaire, have indicated that their regional contributions to collective security were in a sense an implementation of Article 43.

3. As recommended by the Collective Measures Committee to the Ninth General Assembly, the United Nations should assist any regional organization in resisting aggression. Regional organizations should have an equal obligation to assist the United States in resisting aggression.

4. Regional organizations should have the same relationship to the United Nations as contained in the Atlantic Pact and the Greek-Turk-Yugoslav agreement in which the regional resistance is merged with United Nations resistance when the United Nations acts.

5. A regional agreement, if it is to be truly one for collective security and not an alliance, must be directed against aggression from any source. (To all the signatories except the United States, the Southeast Asia Treaty Organization is directed against aggression as such. The United States, as far as its own commitments are concerned, has interpreted the pledge against aggression in this treaty to be

directed against Communist aggression only. Thus, to many people abroad the United States views SEATO as a strictly anti-Communist alliance.)

6. The members of any regional organization should agree to modify the terms of the organization when they are found, by a vote of any seven members of the Security Council or a two-thirds vote of the General Assembly, to be inconsistent with the principles of the United Nations.

Regional arrangements must be placed in a subservient position to the United Nations. The United Nations cannot afford to permit any regional organization to have equality with it. This is a difficult statement to make, particularly since the inter-American system antedates the United Nations. Nevertheless, despite qualifications and explanations, the principle should be maintained.

The first conflict between a regional organization and the United Nations arose in the Security Council in June, 1954, over Guatemala. The Government of this Central American republic, threatened by revolt from within and the pressure of organized bands of Guatemalans from without, appealed to the United Nations Security Council and asked it to set up a Peace Observation Commission to watch its borders. The Security Council had before it a resolution, one part of which would refer the question to the Organization of American States; the other part, a French amendment, called for a cease-fire.

All members of the Security Council except the Soviet Union felt that here was a clear case in which Charter procedures provided that the matter be dealt with regionally first through the Organization of American States. The Soviet Union vetoed the resolution. Guatemala, not a member of the Council, could not vote. The Council then passed unanimously the latter part of the resolution which called for a cease-fire.

Some interesting legal points were involved. Guatemala insisted that her complaint was being brought under Chapter VII providing for resistance to aggression, and therefore no appeal to the Organization of American States could be requested. Many members of the United Nations were deeply concerned with this conflict between regionalism and the world organization.

The United States has come very far since the time when it would not accept a pledge accompanying the Versailles Treaty to come to the aid of France along with Britain. It has undertaken obligations under the Charter with fifty-nine other members of the United Nations to resist aggression. It has fulfilled its obligations nobly in Korea. In addition, the United States has obligations of a regional or bilateral nature with forty-three nations. Twenty nations are covered by the Organization of American States. An additional thirteen are covered by the North Atlantic Treaty. Seven others are covered by the Southeast Asia Treaty. The United States, furthermore, has military understandings with Pakistan, Yugoslavia, Turkey and Greece, the last two now members of the Atlantic agreement. The United States also has formal or informal arrangements for the security of the Republic of Korea, Germany, Japan and the Chinese Nationalist Government on Formosa. Thus, the United States has been one of the major bulwarks in the defense of the free world in the postwar period.

One of the most difficult and yet one of the most necessary steps for the United States Government to consider is how, without weakening the efficiency of these arrangements, it can co-ordinate them under the over-all United Nations collective security system. If this can be accomplished the burden upon the United States might be lessened and the suspicion which these arrangements cause in some quarters would be reduced.

Regional security arrangements are needed until a stronger system of United Nations collective security can be developed. They should, however, be developed as contributing factors to the universal system of security. Obviously there can be no certain peace in one part of the world if it can be disturbed by conflict from another. As the threat of war recedes and drastic disarmament takes place, as freedom advances and prosperity comes to the underprivileged parts of the world, the emphasis on political regional arrangements will tend to lessen.

CHAPTER V

Disarmament

Which comes first, disarmament or collective security? The
halls of the League of Nations echoed to both sides of the
argument. In a somewhat different setting the debate goes
on in the United Nations today.

A comparison between the League of Nations Covenant
and the United Nations Charter on these subjects is interesting. It will show that the Covenant was more precise on
disarmament and the Charter more precise on collective
security.

The United Nations Charter contains surprisingly little
specific commitment on disarmament. In contrast, the obligations of the League of Nations Covenant on disarmament
were more positive and binding. Article 1 (2) of the League
of Nations Covenant made willingness to accept arms regulations a price of membership. In addition to giving guar-
antees of its sincere intention to observe its international
obligations, an applicant "shall accept such regulations as
may be prescribed by the League in regard to its military,
naval and air forces and armaments."

The Covenant recognized the influence of armaments on
peace when it said in Article 8 (1) the Council shall "formu-
late plans for such reduction for the consideration and action
of the several Governments." The Covenant further provided that such plans would be subject to reconsideration and
revision at least every ten years. Article 9 provided for a
permanent commission "to advise the Council on the execu-

tion of the provisions of Articles 1 and 8 and on military, naval and air questions generally."

On the other hand, the Charter of the United Nations neither places disarmament as one of the overriding tasks of the organization, nor does it make willingness to agree to disarmament regulations a price of membership. The word "disarmament" first appears in the Charter under Article 11 where it is stated that the General Assembly "may consider the general principles of co-operation in the maintenance of international peace and security, including the principles governing disarmament and the regulation of armaments, and may make recommendations . . . to the Members or to the Security Council or to both."

Under Article 26 of the Charter the Security Council shall be responsible for formulating, with the assistance of the Military Staff Committee, plans to be submitted to the members for the establishment of a system for the regulation of arms. Article 47 provides for the establishment of this Military Staff Committee which shall advise and assist the Security Council "on all questions relating to the Security Council's military requirements for the maintenance of international peace and security, the employment and command of forces placed at its disposal, the regulation of armaments, and possible disarmament." Apparently the regulation of armaments was considered feasible—disarmament "possible."

What is the reason for the difference in emphasis? The First World War, the first to be waged with what then seemed the weapons of modern science, had shocked and startled mankind. The Central powers were disarmed, the Austrian-Hungarian Empire fragmentized. The Soviet Union was scarcely considered a military factor. Disarmament agreement among the heavily armed states, the United States, Britain, France and Japan seemed possible. Indeed, in retrospect, disarmament seems so much easier then

than now that one wonders why the League's plan did not
succeed. One will always wonder whether if an arms agreement had been reached German rearmament could have been
blocked and the tragic history of the postwar years, with
the final catastrophe of the Second World War, avoided.

It has been said that the League of Nations failed because
of the futility of attempting to solve the disarmament
problem by purely technical means while ignoring the prerequisite of a political agreement which should furnish a
guarantee of security against aggression.

The framers of the United Nations Charter profited by
this lesson. They placed collective security first. A series of
collective security articles reached their climax under Article
43 by which the members agree to make available to the
Security Council armed forces and assistance for action
against an aggressor.

It would be a mistake to give the impression that disarmament was not in the minds of the framers of the Charter.
However, the fate of the world for the next years seemed to
be in the hands of the four or five big policemen with permanent seats in the Security Council. If they remained united
they could keep the peace of the world during the reconstruc-
tion period. They could agree among themselves on a reduction of armaments. The building of the organization,
therefore, and the establishment of a system of collective
security seemed to be the first concern of the founders. Consequently, while the first disarmament obligation of the
League Covenant is to be found in Article 1, that of the
Charter is to be found in Article 11, and then in less positive
terms.

However, after the Charter was completed, and before it
went into effect, the United States dropped two atomic bombs
on Japan at a cost of one hundred thousand lives, thus profoundly changing the arms situation. Secretary Dulles, re-

ferring to this situation, said in part: "As one who was at San Francisco in the spring of 1945, I can say with confidence that had the delegates at San Francisco known we were entering the age of atomic warfare, they would have seen to it that the Charter dealt more positively with the problems thus raised."

The four powers, the United States, the Soviet Union, the United Kingdom and France, agreed before the First General Assembly to sponsor a four-power resolution setting up an atomic energy commission. The Baruch Plan for the regulation and control of atomic weapons was presented to the Atomic Energy Commission in 1946. Since that time innumerable meetings of the General Assembly, disarmament commissions and subcommittees have focused on the problems of conventional weapons and weapons of mass destruction and their interrelation.

The conclusion is inescapable that the subjects of disarmament and collective security are interrelated. They must be approached simultaneously. They were not so approached in the time of the League of Nations. France felt deserted because the United States and Britain would not honor their pledges at Versailles that the two countries would go to the aid of France if attacked by Germany. As James T. Shotwell has said, the United States pushed disarmament by mathematical ratio, while refusing to recognize the relationship between collective security and disarmament. And the allied powers on the continent, at least, were too vengeful in memory of earlier wrongs to recognize that their former enemies must in time be brought within a system of collective security.

The nations today cannot disarm unless a substitute for arms is found in collective security machinery for the settlement of disputes and for the enforcement and maintenance of peace. But the rising tide of armaments is a barrier to the development of this collective security machinery. True collective security is impossible so long as the collective forces available to the United Nations are greatly outnumbered by the huge military forces of the heavily armed states.

Today the increasing burden of armaments, as well as adding to international insecurity, is seriously threatening the stability of the world's economic structure which is necessary for peaceful existence. Daily an increased proportion of the world's manpower, raw materials and factories are consumed by military preparedness. Each nation that can afford to do so must experiment at whatever cost to maintain supremacy in new weapons. Few Americans would think of challenging the amount of money that the Atomic Energy Commission must spend to keep ahead in the game of hydrogen and atomic weapons.

And as a greater part of national life becomes consumed by military preparation, the imagination toward peaceful solutions is dulled. Nations are becoming increasingly security conscious—in the United States respect for civil liberties and the protection of the Bill of Rights are gradually being imperiled.

The League of Nations devoted many hours to the subject of disarmament. The late Major General George V. Strong said that the technical work of the League of Nations proceeded very far. General Strong was Chief Military Advisor to the United States delegation during the greater part of the League of Nations Disarmament Conference. He stated shortly after the atomic bomb was dropped that the technical phase of the League's work, essential to the preparation of any disarmament convention, was of permanent value and, in fact, so far completed that not more than three months would be required to bring it up to date.

General Strong died when the atomic bomb was quite new. His statement was made as scientists and military men were crossing the threshold of thermonuclear weapons. The fact remains, however, that when a political agreement can be reached so that the Disarmament Commission may proceed with full confidence, much of the technical work will have already been done for it by the League of Nations.

As has been seen, the advent of atomic warfare in the summer of 1945 projected disarmament as a major consideration of the United Nations from the moment the organization was set up. At first the United Nations had two disarmament commissions; one for conventional weapons, and one for weapons of mass destruction. When the United States was the sole possessor of atomic bombs, the Soviet Union wished one commission to consider both conventional weapons and mass destructive weapons. The United States wanted the items separated into two commissions. Then, as the Soviet Union approached its own successful atomic bomb, it wanted a separation of the two functions. The United States then reversed its position and wanted both to be discussed by the same body.

At present one disarmament commission is dealing with both subjects. It is increasingly evident that they cannot be dealt with separately. If atomic weapons were abolished and nations fell back on so-called conventional weapons and manpower, the Soviet Union would be in a much better military position than the United States. And reduction of conventional weapons would apparently leave the United States in a far superior position with its greater number of weapons of mass destruction. Obviously all means by which armies can kill men and women must be considered as parts of one armament problem.

The original Baruch Plan provided for international inspection and control and United Nations operation of dangerous plants. It also provided for punishment by an international authority, without interference of a veto, of the individual or the nation violating atomic energy agreements. In the Baruch Plan the United States made the most drastic proposals for supra-national authority or world government in one department of human life that any government has ever presented to the United Nations. The Soviet Union objected to United Nations operation of dangerous plants, as well as to international inspection and control. It insisted on inspection by national governments. It wanted punishment for violation to be meted out by the Security Council, where the veto prevails.

The United States has now abandoned its demand for the operation of dangerous plants, but has continued its insistence on rigid inspection and control.

As the cold war grew more serious, disarmament talks did not get anywhere. In 1951 the General Assembly asked the great powers to meet privately to consider some big-power agreement so that the United Nations could get on with disarmament. The powers could agree on but one step, that a disarmament commission composed of the members of the Security Council plus Canada should proceed to hold meetings. Nineteen fifty-one, 1952, 1953 ticked away in a seemingly insuperable deadlock. The British, French, Americans and Canadians clarified their own thinking and perfected their own ideas. They insisted on a foolproof system of inspection and control. They urged a periodic census of arms so the nations would know the level from which they were to reduce. And, finally, they put forward a proposal for the reduction of standing armies which would leave the Soviet Union and the United States with forces between one million and one and a half million, and France and the United Kingdom with forces limited to between seven and eight hundred thousand each.

The Soviet Union continued to repeat with deadly monotony that there must first be the outlawry of the bomb and then simultaneous reduction of armed forces by one third. In the Disarmament Subcommittee in London in the summer of 1954 the same Soviet record was played over and over again.

However, this situation began to change in the early days of the Ninth General Assembly meeting in the fall of 1954. The Soviet Deputy Foreign Minister, the late Mr. Andrei Vishinsky, announced that his Government was willing to accept the British-French draft on the question of timing as the basis of discussion. This was the very proposal which his government had rejected in the summer. The greatest Soviet concession then seemed to be a willingness to agree that there could be some considerable disarmament before outlawry of the atomic bomb takes place. The Soviet representative was not willing to concede, however, that a violator of the atomic energy agreement can be punished other than by the Security Council where the veto prevails.

The problem at the United Nations, as in the days of the League of Nations, is still essentially political. The nations can agree upon a foolproof system of disarmament if a political agreement or series of political agreements clears the way.

What are some of the questions involved in reaching such agreements?

Has the Soviet Union finally decided that the danger of atomic destruction is so great and the possibility of victory so slim that it has nothing to gain and everything to lose from precipitating world conflict? If one assumes that the Soviet drive toward the triumph of world communism is still in force, and war, as a means of achieving this objective, has been abandoned, the struggle may be waged in the context of peaceful pursuits.

If the Soviet has reached this all-important conclusion,

will it then be willing to reach a peaceful stage of coexistence, to use the words of some Western statesmen, or a *modus vivendi,* to use the language of President Eisenhower?

Will the United States succeed in demonstrating to a skeptical portion of mankind, frequently called the neutral bloc, that this country wishes peace without dominating any people against their will. The support of the neutral bloc on the side of United Nations decisions for the maintenance of peace is very important. Most Americans would believe that their peaceful attitude is sufficiently clear that a demonstration is not needed. Nevertheless, too large a portion of the world believes that while the United States does not wish war, it has but one thought, and that is the maintenance of peace by force of arms. Will the United States convince others that those few who, through misguided reasoning, would follow policies in which there would be great risks of preventive war, cannot possibly lead the United States and the world into catastrophe?

Universal enforceable disarmament with collective security is the final answer to the threat of atomic destruction. In the primitive days before the atomic bomb statesmen talked about limited disarmament, or if they were afraid of the word disarmament, they talked about limitation or reduction of arms. From the time that the Czar of Russia called the first Hague Conference of 1899, down to the present meetings of the United Nations Disarmament Commission, the world has witnessed even more terrible weapons of destruction as science and technology have advanced. Each disarmament conference has had those speakers who pointed out the deadliness of modern weapons. The scientists have warned against the possibility of cobalt bombs, a small number of which properly placed and timed could destroy life on the globe. Now mankind faces the final choice of annihilation or disarmament.

The phrase "universal enforceable disarmament" expresses accurately the need of the time. The logic of necessity determines that disarmament to be successful must be universal. It must be universal because the destruction let loose by modern weapons could be universal. It must be universal because one nation could let loose a chain reaction of destruction that would not stop until the world was consumed. It must be universal because each new weapon of mass destruction fundamentally changes the security calculations of all of mankind.

If disarmament is to be universal, it must be enforceable. It must be guaranteed disarmament. No nation can afford to run the risk of trusting to a disarmament agreement unless provisions exist for the detection and the punishment of the violator be he an individual or a nation.

In these somber days, the greatest reason for believing that the United Nations may succeed in reaching a disarmament agreement is that the danger of mass suicide from atomic weapons is so great that the nations may choose to avoid it by taking comparatively drastic steps for salvation. When man is close to eternity the basic issue may seem clear, with confusing issues swept aside. It may be that armaments and war itself are outlawing each other by the fear they inspire in universal destruction. But man cannot live in such a moral vacuum. He must fill it with the positive agreements and deeds of peace.

CHAPTER VI

Technical Assistance

There is abroad in the world a spirit of "kindliness." Thus Hugh Keenleyside, Director-General of the United Nations Technical Assistance Administration, described the spirit behind the various technical assistance programs. These programs, undertaken by one or a number of nations working together, are based upon a desire to help people help themselves.

The idea that one nation can draw upon the skills of another goes back to antiquity. Missionaries were forerunners of technical assistance programs to the extent that they brought medicine and other skills to teach people how to live better lives. The Rockefeller Foundation has provided examples of organized philanthropic technical assistance.

President Truman dramatized the idea of helping people help themselves in his Point Four Program. He brought misery and its relief into world focus by pointing out their relationship to war and peace. Although the United Nations and its specialized agencies had begun such a program, under President Truman's inspiration it has grown until it is considered one of the most important and constructive of United Nations activities.

No United Nations program provides a better illustration of the organization's expansion based upon a liberal application of the Charter. The authority in the Charter for the technical assistance program is to be found in Article 66 (2) which states:

It [the Economic and Social Council] may, with the approval of the General Assembly, perform services at the request of Members of the United Nations and at the request of specialized agencies.

On this authority the Economic and Social Council elaborated a set of "Guiding Principles" to implement Article 66 (2) as follows:

The participating organizations should, in extending technical assistance for economic development of under-developed countries:

1. Regard it as a primary objective to help those countries to strengthen their national economies through the development of their industries and agriculture, with a view to promoting their economic and political independence in the spirit of the Charter of the United Nations, and to ensure the attainment of higher levels of economic and social welfare for their entire population; . . .

The revolt against hunger goes hand in hand with the struggle for independence. Since 1945 six hundred million people have gained freedom from the colonial system. Along with this upsurge is a revolt of almost half of the people of the world against misery. It is to be found wherever people, even those having their national independence, are still borne down by systems of feudalism and exploitation.

Such misery is all the more galling to some countries like India, because they are proud of their rich culture and ancient civilizations which have made so many contributions to the world of today. They are, nevertheless, up a blind alley economically.

Hand in hand with their misery is illiteracy. Approximately half of the world cannot read or write. A great part of mankind has known nothing but hunger for generations. Their lands are impoverished. Corn that in Iowa might rise to the height of a man's head grows only knee high in the exhausted soil of part of Asia. In a very considerable part of the world men and women cannot look forward to a life expectancy of more than thirty-five years.

In this situation communism has an appeal to people who feel that they have something to gain and nothing to lose by embracing it. The price which people pay for the tools and the technology of the Communists is loss of freedom of mind and suppression of their cultural traditions. One wonders how much damage will be done to Chinese family life and culture before the Chinese spirit asserts itself and breaks through the discipline of dialectic materialism.

The alternative promise to the underprivileged people are the programs of technical assistance. They demand no sacrifice of liberty, culture or traditions.

The United Nations Technical Assistance Program is carried out by the United Nations itself and its specialized agencies: the Food and Agriculture Organization, World Health Organization, International Labor Organization, International Civil Aviation Organization, International Telecommunication Union, World Meteorological Organization, and United Nations Educational, Scientific and Cultural Organization. The United Nations Children's Fund, co-operating with the program, is not a participating agency.

An American recently returned from a United Nations Technical Assistance assignment in the Middle East had working for him a team of persons, only 10 per cent of whom came from the United States. Together they solved the following problems: The country faced the problem of a food supply. The population was growing. What was the best diet for its people based upon what they could best raise? The health of the people was important. If malaria was eliminated more people could raise more food. What were the best routes of getting material to market and to the ports for export? The people in the villages badly needed basic education. They must understand more about the tools that were being provided them; they must be able to read the instructions. Their national accounting system was inadequate. Altogether six agencies of the United Nations combined to help a proud and courageous people, who have demonstrated their willingness to fight for freedom, develop economic and social strength.

Originally some of the specialized agencies had a self-subsidized technical assistance program of their own. So did the United Nations proper. As the Expanded Technical Assistance Program struck world imagination and broadened its scope, closer co-operation between the United Nations and the specialized agencies was necessary. The Technical Assistance Board was created to allocate the special funds and co-ordinate the programs.

The appeals for assistance far exceed the money appropriated by the various governments. One of the most heartbreaking tasks of the United Nations is performed by those who must examine the requests for aid of the member states and pare those requests severely. It has a fund of some twenty-five million dollars, but a fraction of the cost of an aircraft carrier. It is a program over which many men must literally hold their breath each year because United Nations officials do not know whether governments will meet their pledges.

From the standpoint of dollars, the technical assistance programs of the United States are much larger than those of the United Nations. The Colombo Plan—one in which five Asiatic powers, all recently liberated from colonialism, have a program in co-operation with other members of the British Commonwealth—also involves a greater expenditure of money.

Although bilateral and regional plans are important, there is a distinct advantage in the United Nations multilateral program. Under this plan most of the members of the United Nations, plus many more, including those

who are to receive the greatest amount of assistance, contribute their mite to the program. In this way all may feel
that they have a share in the determination of the program
and that they can protect themselves from economic imperialism.

Fortunately not all of the technical assistance experts
come from North America or Western Europe. As people
receive help, they want to give help. And it may be that
Indian technicians will have more understanding of the problems of Thailand and be better able to help its people than
an American or an Englishman whose standards are often
impractically high to start with.

Possibly second only to relief from colonialism is the
appeal of the Technical Assistance Program as carried out
by the United Nations, its specialized agencies and
UNICEF. One cannot underestimate its importance. The
extent of the program and the speed with which it can be
applied may in the next decade help save the world from
revolution and Communist expansion.

Now, a new and almost frightening hope has come to the
underprivileged peoples of the world through the possibility
of the peaceful use of atomic energy. The Ninth General
Assembly adopted unanimously the Atoms for Peace Program. This program was first presented to the General
Assembly by President Eisenhower in a moving speech in December, 1953. And eleven months later the General Assembly unanimously adopted a resolution asking the
Secretary-General to call an International Conference on the
Peaceful Uses of Atomic Energy. And at the same time it
provided that the atomic agency, now being worked out
by certain Western powers, should have a relationship with
the United Nations. At the Ninth Assembly the United
States pledged two hundred and twenty pounds of fissionable

material and the British forty pounds of such material. Presumably it will be distributed by the agency to be set up. It is estimated that this amount of material would be enough to activate a considerable number of experimental reactors throughout the world. Thus, it may very well be that certain peoples with primitive economic systems will, within a generation, leap into atomic power without passing through the conventional stages of power developments. The capacities of this new force in speeding plant growth and curbing disease are only a few of the possibilities for development that were outlined in speeches before the General Assembly. Even accepting the warning of the statesmen not to expect too much in the beginning, one must agree that the ultimate changes to be wrought by atomic energy are great.

These changes may have a leveling effect, with a large part of the underprivileged world catching up faster than normally might have been expected. The peacetime use of atomic energy will also have a profound effect in the highly industrialized nations of the West. Some have estimated that within twenty-five years atomic energy may have an effect upon labor, business and the social life of the peoples of the West comparable to the effect of the industrial revolution.

The problems still to be met are great. Only a beginning has been made. While the food production of the West has gained over the population since the war, a large part of the world is hungrier than ever before because population has outstripped food production.

It is not difficult to make recommendations for future programs:

1. There should be recognition by the Western nations of the importance of the multilateral system of technical assistance to the entire world. As far as the United States is concerned it will continue to give a considerable degree of technical assistance directly. However, the Executive Branch and

the Congress should recognize that the United Nations multi-lateral program is equally or more important than the bilateral program. The Congress of the United States must come to see that dollar for dollar an investment in the United Nations program is the more economical because instead of giving it all, American money is matched almost dollar for dollar. If one takes into consideration the contributions toward staff and the facilities of recipient countries, the United States' contribution to the program is about 22 per cent. And it should never be forgotten that the contribution of some other countries, like Norway, is, per capita, larger than the American contribution.

2. As recommended by both the Eric Johnson Committee and the Randall Committee, the United States should give a larger sum to the United Nations Technical Assistance Program. At the same time, the latter committee recommended that other nations increase their contributions to an even greater degree, so that the enlarged American contribution would not be more than 50 per cent of the total money appropriated to the central fund.

3. There should be closer co-operation between the bilateral, regional programs, such as that of the Colombo group, and the United Nations. The Government of the United States should continue the pattern developed in practice by Harold Stassen, Director of the Foreign Operations Administration, which is that Americans in the field under the United States bilateral program will co-operate closely with the United Nations experts in the field.

4. The program for the peacetime use of atomic energy should be a world-wide United Nations program. This was clearly the intention of the President in his address of December 8, 1953. Sufficient opposition developed in Washington that for months there was an ominous silence as to whether the program would be presented in concrete form to the

United Nations. At the Ninth Assembly the program was so presented. The one part of the program, however, in which United Nations participation is not clear is in the nature of the authority for the peacetime use of atomic energy. Certain Western nations, most of them colonial powers, are negotiating about the form of this authority and its relationship to the United Nations—presumably that of a specialized agency or one with a closer integral relationship.

It is unfortunate that the negotiations among the Western powers had to be outside the United Nations and conducted in such secrecy. For example it appears to certain Asiatic, Latin American and African powers as though certain Western nations are attempting to get a monopoly on the raw material which may literally transform the world and use it for exploitation and domination. The falsity of this charge should be removed as soon as possible by making the program clearly and fully one of the United Nations.

5. The appropriations from various governments should be planned farther ahead than on a yearly basis. At the present time the United Nations program is very much at the whim of too many nations' appropriations committees. These committees may, as in the rush of the closing of the Eighty-third Congress, imperil the program altogether.

6. There should be increasing co-ordination of the specialized agencies and the United Nations in this program. Human nature being what it is, a high degree of autonomy is inherent in the attitude of the specialized agencies.

This spirit of autonomy on the part of the specialized agencies is natural enough and, to a point, good. On the other hand, world peace is the major objective of the United Nations and the specialized agencies, and they should be considered as parts of a central organization, working toward a common goal which can only be achieved through economic and social co-operation.

7. The areas of governmental aid and private investment should be more carefully defined and brought into co-operation. The borderline between technical assistance and private investment is not easy to trace, but possibly some of the differences can be explained. In a country such as the United States the Government provides the highways; private initiative provides the automobiles that ride on these highways. Few private firms want to provide a national public health service or an educational system. While the line of demarcation may be shadowy, it may roughly be said that some things only governments can do and some things private investment should do. It must also be recognized that there are some situations where the prospects for private investment are so meager that governmental technical assistance programs must make a basic start before the economic life of the people can be developed to the point where there is inducement for private investment. Investors from nations that have high competition in their private investment systems must realize that many nations are too impoverished to afford competitive systems and that for the time being a degree of government control or state enterprise, not always understandable to North America, is necessary.

In this connection three rules must be observed if private capital is to assist:

The country to be helped must be protected from exploitation.

The private investor must either be guaranteed against nationalization and indirect expropriation or be assured just compensation if nationalization takes place.

He must be able to bring home some of his profits promptly.

8. A considerable portion of the savings from disarmament should go into international development. This idea was embodied in the late Senator Brien McMahon's first disarma-

ment resolution in the United States Senate; it was implied in Senator Flanders' disarmament resolution in 1953. It has been proposed by United States delegates to the United Nations.

Again we return to the modern missionaries—men and women from many countries who have caught the vision of "kindliness"—the vision of helping people help themselves. Its rewards are practical as well as idealistic because in the long run the countries that give the most will reap a rich harvest in expanded opportunities for export and investment. But most important of all, the danger to world peace, the danger inherent in the unrest of the underprivileged peoples of the world, will disappear, and all will be able to stand shoulder to shoulder in support of the principles of freedom. The differences in the richness and the complexities of their civilizations will not be sacrificed to the blessings of modern technology. The doctrine of dialectical materialism will be defeated by the spiritual qualities of the doctrine of kindliness.

CHAPTER VII

Independence, Self-Government and Human Rights

Six hundred million people, one fourth of the world's population, have won their political independence since the war ended. This is one of the most constructive and one of the most revolutionary factors in the present world situation. Another two hundred million are aspiring for self-government or independence. The way in which their claims are met will have much to do with peace and stability in the next ten years.

The idea that colonial peoples could be given their freedom by decision of an organized society of nations began with the League of Nations. It was the objective of the mandates system that certain peoples able to stand on their own feet should be given independence. As a result, Iraq, Lebanon and Syria emerged from the mandates system into national independence in time to be admitted to the San Francisco Conference.

At San Francisco the nations were aware that war had touched everyone. In some cases the mother country, proud of the loyalty of the colonial peoples during the Second World War, had promised them independence at the war's end. The machinery of war, its suffering, its artificial prosperity, its friendly or unfriendly invasion of soldiers touched every part of the world. The colonial world could not slumber after its experience in the Second World War. At San Francisco the powers, aware of this situation, wrote into the Charter obligations to advance self-government and independence which they might not have agreed to in some of their reactionary moods following the war.

Consequently, the United Nations has played an important part in the struggle of colonial peoples for independence. Some of them, such as Indonesia, Israel and Libya, have been helped to independence by direct intervention of the United Nations. Others have gained their independence through a more liberal policy of the colonial powers as when the United States gave the Philippines their independence and the British gave to countries of the Asian subcontinent the right to choose their own status. Of these, India and Pakistan elected to remain members of the British Commonwealth.

Many of the former colonial peoples, whether they achieved their independence through the liberal policies of the colonial governments or through the aid of the United Nations, have taken their place in the United Nations. They have found in the world organization, particularly in the General Assembly, an opportunity to exercise their newly found freedom. They have also found in it a means for the gradual improvement of their economic and social conditions as well as a place to protest against colonialism remaining in other parts of the world. The vigor with which they play their role in the United Nations shows what the organization means to them in achieving equality and safeguarding their independence. Some of their representatives—Pakistan's Sir Mohammed Zafrullah Khan, India's Madame Pandit, Israel's Abba Eban and others—have been among the most forceful personalities to be found in United Nations debates. They do not always share the views of Western statesmen on the relative importance of world problems before the United Nations. In their estimation, relief from colonialism, advance-

ment of human rights and technical assistance should be
placed ahead of collective security.

The United Nations deals with the problems of colonialism
in a number of ways. First the presumption of the Charter
is that nations will work for independence or self-government.
It was agreed in Article 2 of the Charter to develop friendly
relations among nations based on the principles of equal
rights and self-determination of peoples. It is further stated
as an obligation under Chapter XI that the nations having
colonial territories under their control will agree "to develop
self-government, to take due account of the political aspira-
tions of the peoples, and to assist them in the progressive
development of their free political institutions, according to
the particular circumstances of each territory and its peoples
and their varying stages of advancement."

The United Nations further deals with colonial peoples in
the General Assembly. Occasion has been found in previous
chapters to refer to the growth of the General Assembly as
the paramount body of the world organization. The Charter
defines the scope of activities of the General Assembly as so
broad that any subject comes under its purview. The General
Assembly may discuss any question relating to the matters
of international peace and security brought to it by any
member or by the Security Council or by a state which is not
a member. The General Assembly, according to Article 10,
also ". . . may discuss any questions or any matters within
the scope of the present Charter. . . ."

Hand in hand with these specific means of promoting self-
government provided for in the Charter, the General Assembly furnishes a forum where states that have recently won
their independence may champion the cause of those that
have not. The legal issues may be cloudy, but the spirit is
bright. Some of the colonial powers may claim that for the
Assembly to discuss colonial problems is a violation of

Article 2 (7) which provides that bodies of the United Nations shall not interfere with matters essentially of domestic concern. France may claim that North Africa is its domestic concern. But the fact remains that in the forum of the United Nations there is no untouchable or taboo subject. Those who have not yet won their independence and admission to the United Nations will have plenty of champions in the General Assembly. Colonialism is dying and freedom is on the march. If it were not for the forum of the United Nations these explosive forces might already have torn the world apart. The capacity of the Assembly to debate and serve as a safety valve and point the way to solutions, if not to implement or enforce, is the means by which potentially explosive situations can be channeled into the paths of peace.

In one instance the General Assembly acted as a legislative body in dealing with some of these dependent areas. The Treaty of Peace with Italy provided that if the great powers were unable to determine the future of the Italian colonies, the matter would be decided by the General Assembly. The Assembly in one of its finest hours rejected as too reactionary a plan submitted by the United Kingdom and strongly supported by most of the Latin American countries. At another meeting of the Assembly a more ideal program was adopted. This resulted in independence for Libya after a period of administration by the United Nations, trusteeship with independence in ten years for Somaliland and an autonomous Eritrea joined to a greater Ethiopia.

Another way in which the United Nations helps the colonial peoples is to be found in procedures growing out of Chapter XI of the Charter. This chapter provides that governments that rule over dependent areas must file a report annually with the Secretary-General. The report contains statistical and other technical information relating to economic, social and educational conditions in the non-self-governing areas. The General Assembly voted to set up a committee, whose term it has repeatedly extended, to review the reports submitted to the Secretary-General and make recommendations for improvement. This committee is set up according to the principle of the Trusteeship Council. Each power with non-self-governing territories sits on the committee together with an equal number of representatives of countries that do not have dependent areas.

Here is another illustration of a growing organization. Some of the colonial powers have objected to this procedure on the ground that there is no provision in the Charter for a committee of the General Assembly to evaluate reports submitted to the Secretary-General. Nevertheless, since the General Assembly, like the Security Council and the Secretary-General, may have such agencies as are necessary to enable them to fulfill their functions, there is no reason why such a committee should not be set up. The support for such a committee has found the United States and the Soviet Union voting together in one of the rare instances in United Nations' history.

The United Nations Charter imposes definite obligations for good conduct upon those nations that have United Nations trusteeships. All but one of the old League of Nations mandates have been transferred to the new system. In addition a trusteeship was established for Somaliland. This system is stronger than was the League of Nations mandates system, for the United Nations has its own special body in the form of a Trusteeship Council. This Council contains an equal number of trust and non-trust powers. The right of inspection and the right of petition is provided for. Reports of the trusteeship powers are weighed, petitions examined and inspection teams are dispatched by the Trusteeship Council. The United States is torn between loyalty to the

principle of freedom for dependent peoples and loyalty because of security considerations to its NATO partners, who
comprise most of the colonial powers.

A very basic obligation of trust powers, according to
Article 76 (b) of the Charter, is to "promote the political,
economic, social and educational advancement of the inhabitants of the trust territories, and their progressive development toward self-government or independence as may be
appropriate to the particular circumstances. . . ." Chapter
XII further imposes upon the trust powers the maintenance
of equality without distinction as to race, sex, language or
religion.

The distinction between the exercise of independence and
self-government is a difficult one to make and the need for one
or the other sometimes difficult to evaluate, particularly so
since many people want the maximum independence and feel
that the lesser, self-government, is a sacrifice. Some nations,
such as Eritrea, are not strong enough economically to be
independent in the sense of having their own tariffs and other
attributes of a modern autonomous state. Eritrea is better
off as a self-governing member of a Greater Ethiopia than
if it were to maintain independent statehood. And one might
ask the question whether Italian Somaliland will be ready
for independence at the end of her temporary ten-year
trusteeship.

There is need for a degree of self-control on the part of the
recently liberated peoples. Freedom brings responsibility.
Arab states that refuse to recognize the right of Israel to
exist are scarcely in a position to demand freedom for other
Arab parts of North Africa. Their agitation in Tunis and
Morocco is considered by many as an irresponsible action
that fails to advance the cause of independence or self-government. Another criticism made of the newly freed peoples
is that they are so anxious to struggle against any vestiges of

Western colonialism under which they have suffered in the past that they take no notice of a new imperialism—that of the Soviet Union, which has enslaved a very considerable portion of the human family.

In spite of the problems still to be solved, it is the contention of this book that without the absorptive capacity of the United Nations, without its providing a forum to seek redress or air grievances on the part of colonial peoples, the world might well have exploded. The wisdom with which the United Nations helps the colonial powers give self-government or independence to those who still have not won freedom will have much to do with the peace of the world.

The Charter of the United Nations places human rights and the dignity and worth of the human person as one of its first objectives. As the delegates sat down at the San Francisco Conference the war was being fought against an enemy whose conduct for years was known above everything else for its degradation of the human person.

Early in the Charter international co-operation for the furtherance of human rights and fundamental freedoms is mentioned as one of the purposes of the Organization. Following, various articles of the Charter contain affirmative obligations. As was previously stated, members of the United Nations having responsibility for non-self-governing peoples accept obligations which mean a greater enjoyment of human rights. Under Chapter XII establishing the international trusteeship system, one of the obligations of the trust powers is to encourage respect for human rights and fundamental freedoms for all without distinction as to race, sex, language or religion. Inhabitants of trust areas have the right to petition the Trusteeship Council for redress of grievances.

However, fundamental freedoms and the dignity and

worth of the human person are not only matters for dependent peoples. Indeed, Article 55 establishes a link between
conditions of stability and wellbeing with advancement of
equal rights and self-determination for all peoples. And all
members of the United Nations pledge themselves to take
joint and separate action in co-operation with the United
Nations for the achievement of the purposes set forth in
Article 55. Article 68 of the Charter instructs the Economic
and Social Council to establish a commission for the promotion of human rights. There is no area of mankind that
can be excused from the enjoyment of these fundamental
freedoms.

The disappearance of Nazi tyranny has been followed by
the expansion of Communist tyranny. In a considerable area
of mankind truth is whatever doctrine best serves the state;
spiritual values are sacrificed for dialectic materialism; and
the classic freedoms as we know them are denied.

In the face of this situation, the United Nations has
struggled, and in some instances with great success, to fulfill
the obligations of the Charter. The most signal success is the
adoption of the Universal Declaration of Human Rights by
the Assembly meeting in Paris in 1948. This Declaration was
adopted by forty-eight affirmative votes, none opposed and
eight abstentions. It sets a common standard not only for the
member states, but for "all peoples and all nations."

The Declaration itself was not to be ratified and therefore
not to become a binding international agreement. Nevertheless, it has come to be a source of law because of the way in
which it has been implemented. A covenant on human rights
was to follow the Declaration, but as nations find it more and
more difficult to agree upon the covenants they are more and
more falling back on the Declaration as a way to fulfill the
obligations of the Charter to advance human rights. Portions
of it have been included in the constitutions of new govern-

ments. It has been referred to in resolutions of the Assembly
and other United Nations bodies. It has been cited by national courts and legislatures. In the perspective of history
the Universal Declaration of Human Rights may be known
as one of the most important steps that the United Nations
has taken in its first decade.

In preparing to draft the covenant to follow the Declaration, the Western powers assumed that it would contain those
classic human rights contained in the United States Bill of
Rights and similar documents of the West. However, the
underprivileged peoples of the world argued that the right to
eat was as important as the right to vote, and with their
centuries of misery and exploitation they insisted upon in-
clusion of clauses guaranteeing economic rights. It was the
view of Mrs. Franklin D. Roosevelt as Chairman of the
Human Rights Commission and others that important as
economic rights might be they could not be stated with
sufficient precision to become ratified and part of international law. However, it was finally agreed that there be two
covenants, one containing civil and political rights and the
other economic and social rights.

While these were still being drafted, the United States
Government announced at a meeting of the subcommittee of
the Senate Judiciary Committee considering the Bricker
Resolution that it would not submit the human rights
covenants when completed to the Senate, taking the position
that there were better ways than the treaty method to advance human rights. By this act the United States reduced
its capacity to influence the documents in the drafting stage.

The government attempted to compensate for its advance
rejection of the uncompleted covenants by submitting some
proposals to the Human Rights Commission, including the
establishment of national committees on human rights. These
committees would make annual reports to the United Nations

on conditions in their countries, presumably with the Declaration as the standard of judgment.

Various bodies of the United Nations have been dealing with the advancement of human rights on a case-by-case basis. An attempt has been made to expose the violations of human rights in the totalitarian countries, and *ad hoc* committees on forced labor have piled up a terrible array of facts regarding forced labor in the Cominform Communist countries particularly. The International Labor Organization and other specialized agencies have been promoting human rights in their special fields.

Consequently it will be seen that the United Nations is moving forward on a broad front in an endeavor to achieve the obligations of the Charter to advance the dignity of the human person on a broad basis.

CHAPTER VIII

Membership

The most pressing problem confronting the United Nations in the view of many people is how to bring more of the members of the family of nations into the United Nations. The Secretary-General, in his report to the Ninth General Assembly, said:

. . . Almost half the countries of Europe are absent from the council tables. It is inevitable that the effectiveness and influence of the United Nations are lessened by this fact, not only as regards the questions of direct concern to Europe, but other problems, too, where the experience of the European peoples would make possible a great contribution towards their solution. This consideration applies also to the peoples in other parts of the world who do not yet have the representation in the United Nations to which their role in world affairs entitles them.

It is a serious matter indeed to have such a substantial part of Europe absent from the world organization. An even more baffling problem is presented by the fact that one fourth of the human family is represented by a government in exile.

Two opposing theories of membership were considered by the San Francisco Conference and are compromised in the Charter. One was the idea of a universal organization to which all nations would automatically belong. The other was that of an organization whose membership would be limited by good conduct.

The first United States draft of a United Nations charter,

written by a committee* under the chairmanship of Under
Secretary of State Sumner Welles, contained the following
paragraphs:

1. The membership of the International Organization shall reflect
the universal character of the international community.

2. All qualified states and dominions shall be members of the
International Organization. The Council shall decide as to the
nature of the qualifications.

Presumably all states members of the family of nations
were automatically to belong to the United Nations. True,
the Council was to decide upon the nature of the qualifications, but the qualifications were understood to be technical,
such as what constitutes a state. Moral qualifications were
not involved. A working paper submitted to the Welles Committee for which the author of this book was responsible
stated:

The United Nations might be compared to some individuals in the
frontier community who have acted as vigilantes to suppress lawlessness. While they are suppressing such lawlessness they have
decided to establish a reign of law and order with means of law
enforcement and obligations of good behavior binding upon all
nations whether they wish to consent or not.

This was the universal concept of membership. All nations
were to be bound by the Charter. There could be no escape.
A nation could be denied the benefits of the community because of aggression, as an individual is denied the benefits of
his community if he is guilty of an offense. But the idea of
admission, expulsion and withdrawal was not recognized.

Opposing the theory of universality was the belief that
the United Nations should be an organization of states that

* This committee of private citizens met at the State Department in
1942-43. It was composed of James T. Shotwell, Isaiah Bowman, Hamilton
Fish Armstrong, Benjamin V. Cohen and Clark M. Eichelberger.

have demonstrated their willingness and capacity to sub-
scribe to certain moral standards before admission, unless,
of course, they were charter members of the organization. A
nation must apply; it may be admitted; it may be rejected;
and it may be expelled.

The Charter represents a compromise between the two
theories of membership. The spirit of the Charter and sub-
sequent resolutions of the General Assembly anticipate universality. The obligations of the Charter, as far as the
maintenance of peace are concerned, are binding upon all
nations according to Article 2 (6) whether members of the
organization or not. That article provides: "The Organization shall ensure that states which are not Members of the
United Nations act in accordance with these Principles so far
as may be necessary for the maintenance of international
peace and security."

However, the provisions of the Charter contain standards
of good conduct for membership. They provide:

1. Membership in the United Nations is open to all other peace-
loving states which accept the obligations contained in the present
Charter and, in the judgment of the Organization, are able and
willing to carry out these obligations.

2. The admission of any such state to membership in the United
Nations will be effected by a decision of the General Assembly upon
the recommendation of the Security Council.

Fifty states, belligerents in the war, were represented at
the San Francisco Conference and are original members.
In addition, a place was reserved for Poland as an original
member. Nine nations were admitted to membership through
1950. These are: Afghanistan, Iceland, Sweden, Thailand,
Pakistan, Yemen, Burma, Israel and Indonesia. Five of this
number are former colonies totaling considerable population.
Indonesia, for example, is the world's sixth largest population unit.

As long as the cold war did not interfere too sharply, the admission of new members was possible. But as the cold war extended, it froze the membership situation, as it did other subjects in the province of the Security Council.

Fourteen states which have been able to secure a two-thirds vote of the General Assembly have been blocked by a Soviet veto in the Security Council. Applicants desired by the Soviet Union, have not been admitted because they could not get the required majority of the Security Council.

With cynical indifference to the overwhelming majority of the members of the United Nations and even to treaty obligations to admit certain former enemy states, the Soviet Union is primarily responsible for this block in the membership situation.

The membership of most of the specialized agencies is larger than that of the United Nations because the Soviet veto cannot keep new members out. It is also noteworthy that several Soviet satellites, while being blocked for membership in the United Nations, have been admitted to specialized agencies.

In 1946 the United States looked toward universality by suggesting that all states that had up to then applied for admission be admitted en bloc. The Soviet Union opposed, taking the position that each state should be considered individually. The following year the Soviet Union proposed a package admission of five applicants after the peace treaties with Italy, Finland, Hungary, Rumania and Bulgaria had come into force. Now it was the turn of the United States to say that each applicant should be considered on its merits. This point of view was backed by an advisory opinion of the International Court of Justice which was sought by the General Assembly.

The twenty-one applicants which have been denied admission are: Albania, People's Republic of Mongolia, Jordan, Ireland, Portugal, Hungary, Italy, Austria, Rumania, Bulgaria, Finland, Ceylon, Republic of Korea, Democratic People's Republic of Korea, Nepal, Viet-Nam, Libya, Democratic Republic of Viet-Nam, Cambodia, Laos and Japan. Nine applicants are from Europe. Two applicants are from the Middle East. Ten applicants are from Asia.

Two of the ten applicants are Soviet puppet regimes which have been engaged in an effort to destroy the legitimate governments in power which are recognized by much of the world. These two are the Democratic People's Republic of Korea and the Democratic Republic of Viet-Nam. Another Asiatic state seeking admission to the United Nations is the Outer Mongolian People's Republic. In 1946, the United States Government, while expressing its misgivings with regard to the Mongolian Republic, would have included it in its en bloc admission. Entirely apart from the good conduct qualifications of the Charter, it would be a moot question as to whether or not this government is sufficiently recognized as a state to qualify for membership.

Fourteen states have been endorsed for membership by resolutions of the General Assembly as a demonstration to the Security Council and to the world that the majority of the members of the United Nations would like to have these countries admitted. There have been a number of impressive demonstrations in the Assembly, particularly in the case of Italy. However, these expressions of the will of the Assembly have had no effect upon the determination of the Soviet Union to cast a veto in the Security Council.

The General Assembly has debated at length on what could be done to break the deadlock over the admission of new members. It has appointed committees to examine the question and use their good offices, but to no avail. No formula has yet been found to overcome the imperturbable Russian delegates who veto fourteen applicants for admission as a means of pressure for the admission of Soviet satellites.

What are the alternative measures that might be considered?

One is the acceptance of a "package deal." Quite obviously this deal could not include certain puppet, Communist, revolutionary regimes set up for trouble-making purposes, such as the Democratic People's Republic of Korea and the Democratic Republic of Viet-Nam. But most of the twenty-one applicants could seriously be considered for an across-the-board agreement.

The latest Soviet proposal for a "package deal" encompassed fourteen states: Ireland, Portugal, Austria, Italy, Finland, Albania, Hungary, Bulgaria, Rumania, Transjordan, Libya, Mongolian People's Republic, Ceylon and Nepal. This arrangement, while bringing in four Soviet satellites from Europe as well as the Mongolian People's Republic from Asia, would bring in four important free nations of Europe, two from the Middle East, as well as Ceylon and Nepal from Asia.

One problem in making such a deal is whether the majority of the Assembly would have to pay the Soviet a price later on for securing the admission of Japan, the Republic of Korea, Viet-Nam, Cambodia and Laos, and the Federal Republic of Germany.

If some arrangement could be made by which the Soviet Union and the Western nations would agree to admit a substantial portion of the applicants, it would be in line with the report of the Secretary-General to the Ninth Assembly in which he states: " . . . If it does not seem possible to break the present log-jam all at once, a beginning might be made with some of those cases which do not directly enter into the balance between the conflicting camps."

Twice the International Court of Justice has been asked for an advisory opinion. The first query to the Court in 1947 concerned the basis of a "package deal" itself. Can a member " . . . subject its affirmative vote to the additional

condition that other states be admitted to membership in
the United Nations together with the applicant?" The Court
found no. There were no additional qualifications for membership except those contained in the Charter.

A more drastic alternative is to try to find some way
around the veto on membership in the Security Council as
the nations were able to find a way around the veto in cases
of aggression.

The reasons for such an effort are overwhelming and grow
increasingly so. The use of the veto as an instrument of
national policy by the Soviet Union is clearly in violation of
the spirit of the San Francisco Conference and of the explanations made when the veto was inserted. Almost half of the
vetoes that have been cast in the Security Council have been
to prevent the admission of new members.

We must go back to the intention of the framers of the
Charter. The late Secretary of State Stettinius clearly states
that the reason for the Security Council veto in substantive
matters is because decisions taken by it might lead to
measures under Chapter VII. And this chapter, providing
for the restraint of aggression, might involve disproportion-
ately large contributions on the part of the great powers
to enforce the peace. He did not mention admission of new
members in this connection.

After weeks of tension, in which the San Francisco Conference, according to the late Senator Vandenberg, came nearly
to the breaking point, the formula for voting in the Security
Council was agreed upon. The great powers made statements
to the effect that the veto was to be used sparingly. It was
presumed that there would be friendly discussion among the
five great powers so that their unanimity would be foreshadowed in important cases.

The necessity of admitting new members to the United
Nations is very clear. If Italy and Austria, if Japan and

Ceylon and Ireland and other nations cannot be admitted, the tendency for alliances and blocs outside the United Nations will increase. The moral foundation of a peaceful international society cannot be furthered unless many more members of the human family are admitted. The Charter is binding upon all members of the community of nations so far as the obligations of peace and war are concerned. The presumption is that they should have an opportunity to participate in the organization based upon such law.

For some time Argentina and several other states have argued that paragraph 2, Article 4 of the Charter did not mean that the Security Council recommendation to the General Assembly must be favorable, that it was sufficient for purposes of action by the General Assembly if the Security Council had made a favorable or unfavorable recommendation.

Under the influence of this necessity in November, 1949, the General Assembly asked the International Court of Justice for a second advisory opinion on the question of admitting new members "when the Security Council has made no recommendation for admission by reason of the candidate failing to obtain the requisite majority or of the negative vote of a permanent Member upon a resolution so to recommend."

The argument centered on the point that if the Security Council had failed to recommend favorably because of a negative vote or veto, could the vote be considered a recommendation not to admit, in which case could the General Assembly proceed to admit a state after considering a negative recommendation?

Another issue involved was, if a candidate in the Security Council fails to receive a vote in favor of admission, can such a negative action be considered a negative recommendation?

The Court found by a vote of twelve to two, first, that it is impossible for the General Assembly "to attribute to a vote of the Security Council the character of a recommendation when the Council itself considers that no such recommendation has been made." And therefore the Court was of the opinion that membership of a state "cannot be effected by a decision of the General Assembly when the Security Council has made no recommendation for admission, by reason of the candidate failing to obtain the requisite majority or of the negative vote of a permanent Member upon a resolution so to recommend."

The arguments of the two dissenting judges were persuasive. Señor Alvarez argued that a situation could arise in which admission of a state had been approved by all members of the Security Council except one and by all of the members of the General Assembly except one and still not be admitted. This, he said, would be reducing the United Nations to an absurdity. In fact, something approaching this absurdity has happened, for in fourteen instances the admission of a state has been favored by all members of the Security Council except one and by an overwhelming majority of the General Assembly.

Señor Alvarez also said, "It is consistent with the spirit of the Charter by the terms of which the U.N.O has a universal role, with the consequence that all members of the international community which fulfill the conditions laid down in Article 4 should be admitted to the United Nations; these States have a *right* to be admitted."

Here again the dynamics of the international situation point toward universality in the face of the restrictive behavior of the Security Council in the question of membership.

It is the writer's contention, therefore, that given the intention of the framers of the Charter that the veto was to be used sparingly and not as an instrument of national pol-

icy; and given the fact that the admission of new members
is of such vital importance, the United Nations General
Assembly would be justified in declaring its right to admit
new members upon a recommendation, either favorable or
unfavorable, of the Security Council.

How could this be done? The Security Council or its
chairman could report to the General Assembly that the
Council was recommending unfavorably because the veto
had been cast or a majority of seven not secured. The General Assembly then could declare that it had the right to
accept or reject the recommendation of the Security Council
and could reject it and admit the applicant. This is an
interpretation of the Charter that was supported by a committee of experts at the San Francisco conference.

Such a step, like the Uniting for Peace Resolution, would
acknowledge a profound change in the functioning of the
United Nations by which two bodies originally placed on
the same level have lost this juxtaposition.

Several stop-gap measures have been proposed.

Roscoe Drummond, head of the Washington Bureau of
the New York *Herald Tribune*, has made an original suggestion to deal with those numerous states, particularly in
Western Europe, which have been deprived of membership
because of the Soviet veto. Remarking that representatives
of some of these states are to be seen in observers' seats in
the Assembly Hall, he has suggested the following: The observers of states not members of the United Nations should
meet regularly in one of the committee rooms and debate the
items on the Assembly agenda. Mr. Drummond goes further
and suggests that they organize themselves after the pattern
of the United Nations itself with both a Security Council and a General Assembly. Their conclusions would be
presented to the United Nations by the United States or
some other sponsor. There would be several advantages in

this plan. Their discussions would give these nations a sense of participation in the United Nations; their views would be known; and their constant presence would be added pressure for their eventual admission.

At the Ninth General Assembly the United States was contemplating a proposal to go further and admit those states capable of security a simple majority of seven in the Security Council and a two-thirds vote of the General Assembly to the Assembly floor where they would speak and debate without the right to vote. The United States proposal was not formally presented because of opposition on the part of many states who felt that the procedure was neither wise nor legal.

The case of Communist China will not let the Assembly and its members rest. China is a member of the United Nations, so that technically the question is a procedural one: Shall the Credentials Committee continue to accept the credentials of the delegates of the Government in Exile of Nationalist China? Or shall this Committee accept the credentials of the delegates of the Chinese People's Republic now in control of the Chinese mainland? In the eyes of many people the issue transcends technicalities and assumes the importance of admitting a new member.

Nowhere does the clash between the principles of universality and exclusiveness become more clearly in evidence. Many anti-Communist delegates from Western Europe argue that it would be much better to have the Peiping delegation in the United Nations than outside. In the United Nations it can be talked to and watched; outside it is almost beyond diplomatic contacts. They argue further that if the Peiping Government is to develop any independence of policy from the Cominform, it must be given an opportunity to associate with other nations in the organized world community. Under the present circumstances its policy cannot escape Soviet orientation. The Communist Government, much as it may be disliked, is the effective government in control in China and, as such, should be accepted in the United Nations.

Some of those who argue for the representation of Communist China assert that had the Peiping delegates been seated in the United Nations in the spring of 1950, and had United Nations forces not gone to the Yalu River, the Chinese Communists might never have entered the struggle and collective security would have achieved its victory with minimum losses and little friction.

The counter argument is that it is repugnant to admit the Peiping delegates when their Government is still in a state of aggression vis-à-vis the United Nations and when it refuses to agree upon reasonable terms for United Nations–supervised elections in Korea. The Peiping Government is responsible for many thousands of United Nations casualties and until it is willing and demonstrably capable of fulfilling the obligations of the Charter its delegates should not be seated.

It is essential above all that the United Nations move toward universality. When a Charter review conference is held it can unravel the compromise in the Charter between universality and exclusiveness. It would seem that it would be best for the United Nations to go back to the original concept of membership as agreed to by the Sumner Welles Committee in 1943 and incorporate the provision providing for automatic universal membership.

However, years may go by before such a conference can be held successfully. Meanwhile every effort should be made to admit as many new members as possible. And if cold war tension relaxes an effort should be made to secure an Assembly resolution pledging the United Nations to the principle of universality in practice even before it can be written into the Charter.

CHAPTER IX

Charter Review

Any constitution can be revised with profit at the right time. What is the right moment for the General Assembly to call a review conference with the object of revising the United Nations Charter?

It is the history of constitutions that in a moment of idealism and crisis a people adopt a rule of conduct which may be difficult for them to live up to when the heroic mood passes. And then there comes a period of time in which people are forced to follow rules of conduct which they would not adopt if they were to write their constitution at that time.

Today the American people are in an ebb-tide of devotion to civil liberties as the result of preoccupation with Communist subversion. Would they today, without qualifications, adopt their Bill of Rights which was written into the Constitution in 1791?

The reactionary mood passes and then in a wave of idealism or impelling necessity people again rise to a heroic mood and advance their constitution a step farther. So mankind advances, holds the line, sometimes retreats and advances again.

There are of course exceptions to this picture. Such serious flaws may be found in a constitution that its subjects have to make some improvements even when the tide of idealism is running out. But in the main the basic documents should be rewritten when the tide of idealism is rising.

The timing of a conference to revise the United Nations

Charter is a delicate problem. The wisdom of holding a conference should not be confused with the desire to improve
the Charter. And those who caution care in timing must not
be accused of being opposed to revision itself.

In the tenth year of the United Nations, the world is in
an ebb-tide of idealism and sacrifice toward it. Public opinion
is as basically in support of the United Nations as the only
hope for peace as it was nine years ago. But at the moment
the mood is not toward ". . . a more perfect union. . . ." It
could change overnight. Increasing fear of hydrogen destruction and a sudden revival of idealism might make review
and revision possible and desirable immediately.

The Charter of the United Nations provides that the
Tenth General Assembly shall discuss the question of a review
conference. It can call such a conference by a majority vote
including any seven members of the Security Council. A
review conference to be called by any other Assembly must
have a two-thirds vote and seven members of the Security
Council.

The Secretary of State, John Foster Dulles, has announced
that the United States will support a review conference to
be called by the Tenth Assembly. He outlined areas for
public study. The Chairman of the Senate Foreign Relations
Committee in the Eighty-third Congress, Alexander Wiley,
was Chairman of a subcommittee that held hearings on the
subject throughout the country.

The Eighth Assembly, in anticipation of a review conference, authorized the publication of unpublished documents
of the San Francisco Conference. However, no noticeable
enthusiasm for such a conference was in evidence on the part
of other delegates, except for some from South America.
Practically nothing was said on the subject at the Ninth
Assembly.

There are various attitudes toward a review conference.

Certain groups favor it only when the international and domestic climate is such that its success would be an almost certainty. By a successful conference is meant one that would succeed in improving and strengthening United Nations procedures.

At the other extreme is the school of thought that would have a review conference even if the international climate is not favorable in the belief that the very holding of such a conference would arouse public opinion to a more idealistic mood and thus counter the conservative trend of today.

There are some who oppose a review conference because they believe it would check the evolution of the United Nations toward increasing authority. And one must reckon with those who want a weaker United Nations and either support a conference because it would give them an opportunity to weaken the organization or oppose a conference because they feel it would strengthen the organization.

This chapter proceeds on the thesis, supported by public opinion polls, that the people overwhelmingly want a stronger United Nations to preserve the peace. There are three ways in which this objective can be accomplished.

One is through an improved attitude on the part of governments. This is dealt with in the last chapter of this book.

Another is through a liberal interpretation of the Charter and the addition of new bodies by general agreement. It has already been seen how the Uniting for Peace Resolution found a way around the veto in cases of aggression or threats of aggression. It has been seen how articles of the Charter have been broadened and enriched by implementation and interpretation. A striking example is to be found in the Guiding Principles laid down by the Economic and Social Council to implement Article 66 and thus make possible a technical assistance program vast in concept, if not yet in financial scope. Indeed, if a review conference were to be held in 1956, the statesmen must discuss the Charter and organization of 1956 and not those of 1945. Additional ways have been outlined in which by bold interpretation the nations might further implement the Charter as a living, expanding document.

The addition of new bodies is in a sense an implementation of the Charter growing out of liberal interpretation. The Uniting for Peace Resolution led to the Peace Observation Commission and the Collective Measures Committee. In order to carry out the General Principles of the Technical Assistance Program laid down by the Economic and Social Council, the Technical Assistance Board and Technical Assistance Administration were created. Additional bodies of greater scope and importance such as authorities to regulate the military and to advance the peacetime use of atomic energy are on the horizon.

The final way in which the Charter can be strengthened is by revision of its text. Certainly basic changes might well be made at the appropriate moment.

What are the problems and legal issues involved in revision? The United Nations is neither a league of states nor a world government. Therein lies the dilemma of revision. The United Nations is in the shadowy area between an organization of states and a world government.

The International Court of Justice, in an advisory opinion in 1949, defined the Charter and the nature of the organization in such a manner that the late A. H. Feller, Chief Counsel to the United Nations, compared the opinion to the famous McCulloch versus Maryland decision in United States Constitutional history.

The Court was asked for an advisory opinion as to whether or not the United Nations had authority to claim damages from member or non-member states for losses suffered by its personnel in their territory. After reviewing the various obligations imposed upon the members, the Court concluded:

> In the opinion of the Court, the Organization was intended to exercise and enjoy, and is in fact exercising and enjoying, functions and rights which can only be explained on the basis of the possession of a large measure of international personality and the capacity to operate upon an international plane. It is at present the supreme type of international organization, and it could not carry out the intentions of its founders if it was devoid of international personality. It must be acknowledged that its Members, by entrusting certain functions to it, with the attendant duties and responsibilities, have clothed it with the competence required to enable those functions to be effectively discharged.

The Court went on to say that it had come to the conclusion that the organization was an international personality. The Court made it clear that this conclusion was not the same as saying that the United Nations was a state, still less is it the same thing as saying that it is a super state.

Here, then, is the United Nations, an international personality, clothed by its members with authority to fulfill certain functions effectively and whose members have taken obligations toward it. But it is neither a state nor a world government.

There is a moral distinction if not a legal one in the phrase "We the peoples of the United Nations . . . " with which the Charter opens, as compared to "The High Contracting Parties . . ." which was the opening phrase of the League of Nations Covenant. The Charter of the United Nations differs from the Covenant of the League both in the references to the United Nations as an entity and in a greater limitation on national sovereignty. In the League Covenant it is the members that do this or that. In the United Nations Charter, the "organization and its members" shall act in pursuance of the purposes and principles of the Charter. The "organiza-

tion" shall ensure that non-member states shall be bound
by the peace and security obligations of the Charter. All
members pledge themselves to take joint and separate action
in co-operation with the "organization" in the achievement
of the purposes set forth in Article 55.

The Charter is replete with references to the United Nations as an organization acting in co-operation with, separate
from, or advisory to its members.

Likewise the United Nations Charter imposes upon its
members a considerable pooling of sovereignty. In regard to
peace and war the obligations are specific. The members
shall fulfill in good faith the obligations assumed by them in
the Charter. All members shall settle their international
disputes by peaceful means and in such a manner that peace
and justice are not endangered. All members shall refrain
in international relations from the threat or use of force.
All members shall give the United Nations every assistance
in any action it takes in accordance with the present Charter
and shall refrain from giving assistance to the aggressor.
And when the Security Council, by a vote of seven members
including the affirmative votes of the permanent members,
takes action "the members of the United Nations agree to
accept and carry out the decisions of the Security Council
in accordance with the present Charter."

If any party to a case before the International Court of
Justice fails to perform the obligations incumbent upon it,
the other party may have recourse to the Security Council.
The Council may, if it deems necessary, make recommendations or decide on measures to give effect to the judgment of
the Court.

The relationship of the trust powers to the trust areas is
definitely prescribed.

In the broad field of economic and social co-operation and
human rights the organization is charged with positive

action. And the members pledge themselves to take joint and separate action in co-operation with the organization for the achievement of these ends. Thus, in addition to the precise obligations for the maintenance of international peace and security and the administration of trust areas, the members have subscribed to general principles of good conduct in a broad field.

Basically the argument for Charter revision is broader than the question of the abolition or reduction of the veto. In the free world at least the basic issue is how much additional authority shall the members confer upon the United Nations.

There are those who would revise the Charter to define very clearly certain elements of limited world government or federation. Others believe that to define the supra-national authority in precise terms would be to thwart the natural evolution of the organization. There are those who do not want the United Nations to have an increasing amount of supra-national authority. Indeed, some would kill such international personality as the United Nations now has and reduce it to a league of states.

The argument finds a historical parallel in early American history between the strict constructionists and the liberal constructionists of the United States Constitution. The liberal constructionists won out. So far this has been the experience of the United Nations.

Assuming that a majority of the people want a strengthened United Nations, what are the negative factors that work against such strengthening so far as a liberal interpretation or a change in the text of the Charter is concerned?

The largest negative factor, of course, is the Soviet Union. The Soviet Government has been a strict constructionist; it has been the greatest defender of the text of the Charter stripped of growth and development. It has declared illegal practically every step that has been taken to liberalize the United Nations, such as the Uniting for Peace Resolution. And, undoubtedly, if a review conference were held, it would be the Soviet Union that would attempt to turn the clock back to recreate the unanimity of the five-power system under the Security Council. Undoubtedly the Soviet Union would be against any lessening of the effect of the veto, either in the admission of new members or the peaceful settlement of disputes under Chapter VI of the Charter. It would use a review conference as a forum to declaim against the United Nations as it has grown and developed throughout its first decade.

However, conservative forces are not limited to the Cominform bloc. A movement drastically to reduce the capacity of the General Assembly for unlimited discussion could be expected from some of the colonial powers who object to the freedom with which the General Assembly discusses their dependent areas.

A few years ago it was generally considered that the United States would want a stronger United Nations. Public opinion polls indicate that this is true of the majority of the people. However, lately a movement has arisen which is commonly defined as "Brickerism." This group professes to see in the economic, social and human rights fields of the United Nations an effort to invade American sovereignty.

One wonders if official Washington has had an opportunity, with the numerous other problems confronting it, to think through what it would want to accomplish at a review conference. It will be remembered that the State Department began planning for the San Francisco Conference in the summer of 1942. There were two years' preparation before the Dumbarton Oaks Conference which preceded the San Francisco Conference. A very considerable process developed for the formulation of American views toward the Charter.

No such planning in anticipation of a review conference is going on, although excellent background studies have been made.

The statements of Washington officials indicate both a liberal and a conservative viewpoint toward the Charter. Secretary Dulles took a position in favor of a much stronger United Nations when he spoke of the need for strengthening the disarmament section because of the atomic bomb, and put forward for discussion the idea of a weighted Assembly. On the other hand, he would seem to have thrown his weight against a liberal implementation of the Charter in matters involving human rights and economic and social problems. There are also indications that Washington is moving toward a more "definitive interpretation" of Article 2 (7) dealing with domestic jurisdiction. Such interpretation might make it less possible for the United Nations to concern itself with an ever greater number of subjects, which in the nineteenth century might have been considered matters of domestic concern, but in the atomic age become increasingly matters of world concern.

There are leaders of public opinion here and abroad who fear a review conference lest it provide the protagonists in the cold war with an opportunity to belabor each other. Recent communications from Western Europe indicate that some people fear that the United States wishes a review conference to turn the United Nations into an anti-Soviet alliance. It is feared that a full-dress diplomatic conference in the present climate would simply produce a propaganda forum to air grievances and to score points against each other. The failure of a review conference would intensify bitterness and lead to general disillusionment. In the meantime agitation for a review conference enables people to escape from the reality of present problems by debating how the Charter should be changed.

But there is another side. The argument is very persuasive, assuming a considerable proportion of mankind has maintained its ideals, that a review conference, even if the hour is dark, might shed some light. The very fact of the statesmen meeting might improve the international atmosphere. And the argument is buttressed by the fact that a wide discussion now will mean that millions of people who have not thought about the United Nations for some time would study it. They might make up their minds on how much stronger they would wish to see it become.

It is hard to disassociate the question of a stronger United Nations from the one having to do with the present desirability of a review conference. The writer has been accused by isolationists of advocating world government. At the same time he is frequently accused by advocates of world government as favoring the *status quo* because he indicated that the time might not be right to hold a review conference. Here might be the place to make his position clear, at least at the end of the Ninth Assembly.

Until the tensions between East and West have been drastically reduced and until governments have an opportunity for more careful preparation, a full-dress diplomatic conference would be a propaganda battle which would harm rather than help the United Nations.

On the other hand, the writer is aware of the fact that the way to get peoples and governments engaging in the necessary discussion and planning is to set the date for a conference. Convinced that for the next few years a diplomatic conference might be too dangerous, yet wanting to take advantage of public discussion, he believes that the best procedure might be for the General Assembly to establish a committee composed of all member states to begin a study of the Charter and discussions for its revision. At the same time the Assembly could call upon all governments to establish commissions of government officials and private citizens to get ready for a conference.

When conditions are favorable the review committee could easily convert itself into a full-dress conference. This procedure would take advantage of the fact that the General Assembly at its tenth session can provide for a review conference by a majority vote. Or, the Tenth Assembly could call such a conference for 1958, 1959 or 1960, but establish the committee immediately to do the preparatory work for the conference.

The purpose of this chapter is to discuss the pros and cons of a review conference. This is not the place to go into detail about the various proposals for revision of the Charter.

There are of course certain minimal improvements in it which Americans increasingly recognize as desirable. They concern the veto in the functioning of the Security Council. It is generally believed that the veto should be denied any great power in the selection of the Secretary-General, the admission of new members and in making recommendations for the peaceful settlement of disputes. On the other hand, it should probably be maintained in cases where the Security Council was voting to engage in military action which would involve the use of American troops.

The more drastic revisionists contemplate fundamental changes in the structure of the United Nations beyond the Security Council. They would change the United Nations into a limited world federation or world government. They contemplate, for illustration, a General Assembly with legislative powers. Here the suggestion of Secretary Dulles that the Assembly might proceed by weighted voting has pertinence.

In the view of the writer one of the most important revisions to be undertaken, whether mild or drastic, is to provide for automatic membership without any procedures for expulsion or withdrawal. He also believes that there would be an important symbolism in some form of United Nations citizenship.

Quite obviously it would be unfair to any of the schools of revision to discuss their plans here unless they could be given adequate attention.

No substitute, however, can be found for a more loyal performance on the part of members of the United Nations, particularly the great powers. On this all revisionist schools will agree. The United Nations will succeed or fail, and the decision may not be long in coming, not because of a revision conference called by any particular Assembly, but by how well peoples and their governments fulfill their obligations. Will the nations make the United Nations in fact the foundation of their foreign policy? This is the subject of the last chapter.

CHAPTER X

Attitude of Members

Is the United Nations to be the foundation of foreign policy? Or is it to be an instrument of policy? The answer will determine whether the United Nations will grow or decline in stature.

An examination of the preamble, purposes and principles of the United Nations Charter leads to the inescapable conclusion that a dynamic international society was contemplated. The previous chapter has outlined the obligations of a specific and general nature that members have taken under the Charter. It has called attention to the limitations on sovereignty involved. It has quoted an advisory opinion of the International Court of Justice to show that the United Nations is an international personality, clothed by its members with authority to fulfill certain functions.

It is only necessary to consider the objectives of the United Nations as set forth in the preamble to prove that the United Nations was intended to be more than an instrument of diplomatic choice. Some of these bear upon the elimination of war and the establishment of collective security, such as: "to save succeeding generations from the scourge of war . . . ; to unite our strength to maintain international peace and security; to ensure, by the acceptance of principles . . . that armed force shall not be used, save in the common interest." Other objectives look toward the establishment of a condition of justice: "to establish conditions under which justice and respect for . . . treaties and other sources of international

law can be maintained; to practice tolerance and live together in peace. . . ." Still other objectives look toward
human rights and economic and social advancement: "to
reaffirm faith in fundamental human rights . . .; to promote
social progress . . . ; to employ international machinery for
the promotion of economic and social advancement of all
peoples." The fulfillment of these principles involves something more than the United Nations as an instrument of
convenience.

But the Charter goes further. There is the next phrase:
"have resolved to combine our efforts to accomplish these
aims." If the United Nations is the foundation of policy,
peoples and their governments will feel an obligation to add
to its strength and use it for the settlement of their problems.
Under such a concept the United Nations will inevitably
grow. It will increasingly become a society of peoples bound
together with extensive ties of association; it will transcend
the barriers of narrow nationalism.

If, on the other hand, the United Nations is an instrument
of policy, a diplomatic tool to be used as a convenience and
an organ of propaganda, it will tend to become an instrument of governments, not of peoples. The foreign offices, and
frequently the more timid members of such foreign offices,
will determine at any moment what instrument shall be used
to carry out their policies. This narrow concept of the
United Nations is held by those who lack faith in a consistently expanding international community life. When increasing storms come there would be grave danger that the
United Nations would be bypassed because men of little
imagination would lack the policies and the boldness necessary for success through the United Nations. These men
would fall back on old and tried ways of meeting their world
problems, even though these methods have given them the
major failures of the twentieth century.

The mood of the framers of the Charter at San Francisco was that they were building a society of nations. Certainly the peoples of the world, to the extent that they could lift their eyes from the grime of the battlefield, believed that this time they would succeed where the League of Nations failed.

Accepting the United Nations as the foundation of a nation's international policy does not mean that a nation cannot take a step outside of the machinery of the United Nations and still move consistently within the sphere of the Charter. Normal diplomacy and regionalism are fully recognized in the Charter. However, the presumption is that nations will concert their efforts through the United Nations.

The United Nations has held the nations together by a moral unity which has survived the most revolutionary changes of any decade in history. Without this moral unity the world might have already destroyed itself. There is danger today of the nations weakening this over-all moral fabric upon which the peace of the world depends. This fabric can only be maintained if the member nations treat the world organization as they did in 1945—even more fully than they did then—as the beginning of a growing international society.

Nations must never lose sight of the obligations to combine their efforts. They must continue to believe that common wisdom is found through the pooling of ideas. In the give and take of debate, in the bringing together of experts from many different countries, solutions are found and programs developed which no nation could undertake by itself. The danger is that many nations tend to have fixed positions and no longer believe that truth can be found in common wisdom.

In concerting their efforts nations develop institutions for their common good. Whether it is the Commission on Human Rights or the economic commissions for various regions,

whether it is the Technical Assistance Program or an authority for the development of the peacetime use of atomic
energy, these institutions can only be developed by nations
combining their efforts.

If the United Nations loses its vitality, if it ceases to be
the impelling force that has held the world together for nine
years, one may look for certain signs. One will be the hollow
repetition of high-sounding phrases without any effort to
square conduct with these phrases. Another will be an increasingly fixed position in which nations will not negotiate
in common wisdom. And another sign will be that the statesmen who make decisions, because they have the power, will
absent themselves from United Nations meetings leaving the
repetition of phrases there to less important men.

It is time for some soul searching. It is time for a moral
crusade. It is time for some of the dedication that went into
the educational program between Dumbarton Oaks and San
Francisco. It is time for a revival of the idealism of San
Francisco. An analysis of the roles of various peoples and
their governments in the United Nations shows that few, if
any, nations are fulfilling their obligations to the fullest
degree; that, as General Romulo suggested, they are
". . . deliberately failing to tap its mine of potential power."
One can be charitable and delete "deliberately."

Each nation is half in and half out of the United Nations
to the extent that at times it contributes much to the United
Nations and at other times forgets it or fails to use it. And
frequently in forgetting it or neglecting to use it, the nation
is failing to tap the United Nations' mine of potential power.
France presents a tragic example of the last statement. Had
it been willing that Indo-China be brought to the United
Nations as Indonesia was brought to it a few years previously, the tragic symbol of Dienbienphu might have been
avoided and the disastrous Geneva Conference never held.

Here a policy of timidity in using the United Nations was a great mistake for French national interests.

It is the Soviet Union, of course, more than any power, which has maintained a position of fixed rigidity in the political phase of the United Nations and a position of obstructionism in its other activities. In practically all areas there is that hard rock, that fixed position, that unwillingness to compromise, to negotiate; only willingness to veto. But the rest of the world would be committing a tragic error if it permitted the Soviet Union to take possession of the United Nations' field. Soviet rigidity must be matched by imagination, idealism and increasing activity on the part of the free nations in the United Nations.

The nations recently freed from colonialism are among the quickest to invoke the Charter against the policies of the older governments while being extremely sensitive to criticism of mistakes that they themselves might be making. India, because of her democracy and size and the ability of her Prime Minister, may be said to lead the colonial protest bloc in the United Nations. However, India must bear a heavy responsibility for failure to hold the United Nations plebiscite in Kashmir. When the Indian Government's armed invasion of the independent princely state of Hyderabad was placed before the United Nations, the Indian delegate pleaded necessity and expediency in the familiar language of the West. Indonesia, in her effort to liquidate the rest of the Dutch Empire in the Pacific, would make herself an empire by annexing Western New Guinea instead of advocating trusteeship for this territory.

Possibly this chapter should address itself only to the American people and the American Government. For in an analysis of one's own country and its policies one can be on safer ground. The United States has been in a position to do more for the United Nations than any other great power, and has done so. Anyone who looks at the positive side of the ledger can be very proud of America's role.

The American people were happy to have had a few acres in the heart of their most populous city contributed as a piece of internationalized territory for the capital of the United Nations.

At the time when the United States was the sole possessor of the atomic bomb it offered to scrap its atomic program in return for adequate inspection and control. It made most advanced suggestions for a supra-national government in a specific area when it suggested that an international authority be empowered to punish the nation or the individual violating atomic energy agreements. This without the right of great power veto!

When the North Korean forces crossed the Thirty-eighth Parallel to destroy the Republic of Korea which had been recognised by the United Nations, the United States immediately asked the world organization to authorize and participate in resisting aggression at the Thirty-eighth Parallel. The American people willingly made a disproportionate contribution to the United Nations forces. American casualties were over one hundred thousand.

It was the Government of the United States that conceived of the Uniting for Peace Resolution that shifted the center of gravity from the Security Council to the General Assembly. And the United States has made numerous suggestions to the Collective Measures Committee set up by this resolution, including a study for a United Nations Legion.

The Point Four Program of President Truman became the inspiration for a very considerable expansion of the United Nations program for technical assistance. The Declaration of Human Rights and many other steps which the United Nations has taken have been contributed to in great measure by United States policies and statesmen.

What may be one of the most dramatic challenges of our century was presented to the United Nations by President Eisenhower in his Atoms for Peace Program.

Now for the negative side of the ledger. At the moment when we Americans and our government face very grave problems, particularly in the Far East, one hesitates to make suggestions and criticisms. However, it is because I believe that a growing, expanding United Nations is the only hope for world peace and civilization and because I believe that the United Nations will seldom go faster than the United States is willing to go that I make the following comments. In doing so I shall speak of the American people, their Congress and their Executive interchangeably.

The attitude of the United States toward the United Nations has been, like that of other states, half in and half out. Bold as our policy has been at times, as in Korea, we have not consistently used the full resources and capacities of the United Nations to build a world of peace and security. Support has fluctuated. Sometimes the United States apparently forgets to use the United Nations. Too frequently we expect it to do exactly what we want. At times we fail to use the United Nations for conciliation, but rather as an instrument for propaganda in the cold war. As a people we tend to become disillusioned and impatient.

The United States proposed the plan for the containment of communism with military aid to Greece and Turkey without informing the United Nations in advance of this drastic step. Also, there will always be a considerable section of United States opinion which believes that the Marshall Plan might have been carried out within the framework of or in closer relationship to the United Nations.

The holding of the two-pronged Geneva Conference to unify Korea and to solve the problem of Indo-China outside of the United Nations seemed in the summer of 1954 to have set the pattern for by-passing the Organization in major concerns. The new SEATO, while reaffirming the loyalty of its members to the United Nations, provides for no practical procedural co-operation with it.

At times the United States has exhibited baffling inconsistencies. At one time an outstanding advocate of a convention on genocide and a covenant on human rights, we announced that we would not press for ratification of the Genocide Convention or present to the Senate any human rights covenants when completed. Our retreat on treaties is further illustrated by our refusal even to participate in the drafting of a convention on stateless persons. And although the United Nations is located in the United States, the United States has yet to ratify the Convention on Privileges and Immunities.

Some Americans have a tendency to refer to the United Nations as the hope of the world, but in a rather wistful way, as if the United Nations were the symbol of peace for some distant date and not to be used practically to bring about that peaceful state. We are frequently confused as to what the United Nations is. There seem to be doubts in the minds of some of us as to whether the United Nations is to be a town meeting or the means for the enforcement of collective security, whereas it should be both.

It is unfortunate indeed that so much responsibility must be placed upon one country. Certainly the United States gave lavishly of its manpower and supplies in the Second World War, and lavishly in substance to rebuild the world afterward. But it is the fate of history that our country occupies a position of such strength today that the moral force of the United Nations is no greater than American participation. Other nations will not depend upon the United Nations for the solution of their problems if the United States by-passes it.

What positive attitudes and program could the American people adopt commensurate with these responsibilities?

1. The American people and their government should adopt for their basic thinking the principle that the United Nations is the foundation of American foreign policy. In consequence all United States policies will have an orientation to the United Nations, even those technically carried on outside. This would be in fulfillment of President Eisenhower's declaration that the United Nations is "sheer necessity." Normal diplomacy and regional arrangements will then correspond to United Nations principles.

2. Once that policy is adopted, the problem will be to see that all relevant departments of government carry it out. The President should appoint as officials in all departments dealing with international relations men who consciously believe in the United Nations and, if possible, have had UN experience. This practice should also be applied to the Defense Department.

3. The Assistant Secretary of State for International Organization Affairs, formerly United Nations Affairs, might become an Under Secretary of State for United Nations Affairs. He or an Executive Assistant to the President might be responsible for co-ordinating the relations of all government departments with the United Nations and its specialized agencies. Incidentally, such a program would encourage greater co-ordination of the specialized agencies and the United Nations itself.

4. The United States program of political and military security should be brought within the United Nations framework. As previously suggested, the government should advocate a set of principles governing the relationship of regional arrangements to the United Nations. Likewise, the vast strategic commitments which the United States has

throughout the world should be closely related to the United
Nations system.

5. The Atoms for Peace Program should be carried out
under the United Nations.

6. The United States should give increasing support to
the United Nations Technical Assistance Program.

7. The United States should make stronger its position
of support for self-government or independence for dependent peoples. It should reaffirm its willingness to take joint
and separate action in co-operation with the organization
for the advancement of human rights and fundamental
freedoms.

The position of the United States is a difficult one. It must
be strong, but its strength must be exercised in co-operation
with and in the service of mankind.

It is one of the first nations to approach a predominant
position, some may say the zenith of its power, in a world
partially organized for law and order. Throughout history
nations have risen to dominance in a world of anarchy. There
was little legal or moral restraint upon their conduct. Nations
were not moral persons and they were bound by few laws.
They were checked and checked others in turn by a precari-
ous balance of power.

Today an overwhelming part of mankind is bound by the
legal and moral obligations of the Charter. Nations are tied
to each other through common parliamentary practice and
habit of meeting. Therefore, the leadership of the United
States cannot be exercised outside of or in defiance of this
orderly world community without destroying the community
itself.

A considerable change in the basic concept of foreign
policy is required if nations are to live within the law and
obligations of the Charter. If the United Nations is treated

as an instrument of convenience there will be little inspiration for it to undertake those tasks and establish those precedents which are necessary if peace is to be preserved. If the peoples understand and their governments accept the belief that the United Nations is the foundation of their foreign policy, if they fully understand what it means to "combine their efforts" to develop a dynamic society, then the will of the people can be effective and peace preserved.

In the long run, the success of the United Nations is dependent upon the force of public opinion. Each country must make a vigorous effort to strengthen this opinion. And these efforts must be united so that gradually there will come to be a common conscience, a common thought and acceptance of common standards on the part of the peoples of the United Nations.

Set in Linotype Scotch
Format by Robert Cheney
Manufactured by The Haddon Craftsmen, Inc.
Published by HARPER & BROTHERS, *New York*